Divination has been a part of Chinese culture since the fourteenth century BC. The tradition of the *I Ching* (Yi Jing) is described in the classics, but it is a complex system and often requires the help of specialists. In the same spirit of the *I Ching* it is a method which uses five or six coins to form divinatory numbers. These 'heavenly pennies' are the subject of this book.

Jean Michel Huon de Kermadec, whose *The Way to Chinese Astrology* introduced readers to the astrological traditions, explains the pentagramic or hexagramic numbers formed by the pennies. Through them we can better concentrate our thoughts and understanding. Direct or selfish questions must not be asked of the coins. Advice as to a course of action to take in a given situation rather than the outcome should be sought. Decisions made are still our own.

HEAVENLY PENNIES

Jean-Michel Huon de Kermadec

Translated by
N. Derek Poulsen

UNWIN PAPERBACKS
London · Boston · Sydney

First published in Great Britain by Unwin Paperbacks 1985
This book is copyright under the Berne Convention. No reproduction
without permission. All rights reserved.

UNWIN ® PAPERBACKS
40 Museum Street, London WC1A 1LU, UK

Unwin Paperbacks
Park Lane, Hemel Hempstead, Herts HP2 4TE

George Allen & Unwin Australia Pty Ltd,
8 Napier Street, North Sydney, NSW 2060, Australia

© J. M. Huon de Kermadec and N. D. Poulsen 1985

British Library Cataloguing in Publication Data

Huon de Kermadec, Jean Michel
   Heavenly pennies.
1. Astrology, Chinese
I. Title
133.5'0957   BF1714.C5
ISBN 0-04-133014-5

Set in 10 on 11 point Times by Fotographics (Bedford) Ltd
and printed in Great Britain by Hazell, Watson & Viney Ltd,
Member of the BPCC Group, Aylesbury, Bucks.

Note on Romanisation

Some readers may be puzzled by words such as Yi Jing and Beijing instead of the more familiar I Ching (I King) or Peking. The explanation is that we have employed the system of romanisation of Chinese words known as Pinyin now in force in China and being increasingly used by Western writers and as an aid to teaching Chinese in Western universities.

Contents

Acknowledgements	*page*	ix
Introduction		1
Part I: The Thirty-Two Pentagrams or Divination with the Five Golden Pennies		6
Part II: The Sixty-Four Hexagrams or Divination with the Six Golden Pennies		41
Notes		111
Glossary		114

Acknowledgements

I should like first to express my deep gratitude to Professor François Houang for his co-operation in adapting these popular Chinese divination texts into French. Without his help this work would haven taken much longer and the conclusions been less sure. I know how much his students at l'Ecole Nationale des Langues et Civilisations Orientales appreciate the breadth of his culture and the enriching warmth of his humanity. He understands better than anyone, sometimes to the point of suffering from it, the opposition which exists between the Chinese vision of the world and Western concepts; he is equally aware that they are necessarily complementary.

I also wish to thank my friend Derek Poulsen who is for me much more than the translator of my first book,[1] this one and of those to follow. Our work together on translating into English, our long discussions and his friendly if sometimes severe criticisms have helped greatly to give precision to my thinking. The definitive form of my French texts has benefited much from this collaboration. Both have clearly understood that, however lightweight the subject treated here may appear, it does so only to those who regard divination as a means of learning about the future from a selfish and egotistical point of view. It is quite otherwise in China. There, divination is a moral act which guides us to a better understanding or determination of the best rules of conduct to follow. This book, which complements my first work, is full of lessons about the practical way the Chinese look at life.

I must also thank here our mutual friend John Blofeld whose influence, despite the distance between us, has been decisive for me. In the second part of this work the divinatory numbers are in fact a popular adaptation of the *Yi Jing* and I have frequently referred to his translation.[2] It has also greatly helped my comprehension of a book which, in turn, is so important to an understanding of China. I should love to have translated the *Yi Jing* myself; unhappily for me it would be pointless to do it again.

1 November 1983

Introduction

Those who have read my book about horoscopes will already know how important they are to the Chinese for the self knowledge which can be gained from them. Divination is the earliest religious activity known in China and its principles have remained constant for over 4,000 years.[3] The word 'religious' in this context needs to be explained: it has nothing to do with belief in some supernatural power; rather is it an awareness of the natural laws which rule the Universe. These laws are not personalised, but they have for the Chinese as much reality as gravity or centrifugal force: we can make use of them without understanding their nature. We do no more when we study electricity.

The Chinese are in fact the only true ecologists for they emphasise the need to respect natural laws, or the Universal Order, and they believe that man can accomplish nothing unless he is aware of his relationships in this macrocosm in which, and by which, he has to fulfil his destiny: 'if he does not know his destiny, he will never be a man'.[4] Divination is thus a supremely moral act for it helps us to order our lives in conformity with the laws of the Universe. It must be understood that these laws are the reverse of Manicheism. For the Chinese there are no such entities as 'Good' or 'Evil'. One can sin only by excess or by default for these are sources of disorder which alone can endanger Universal Harmony.[5]

Astrology, acupuncture and the martial arts are all based on the knowledge of the rhythms and relationships which rule our lives and which we must learn to make use of. This is our responsibility to ourselves and to Universal Harmony. The Chinese themselves would certainly not explain their moral ideals in such abstract terms; but I believe that, for our purposes, they summarise adequately the Confucian ethic.[6] If, in the course of seeking guidance by divination, the supplicant wishes to invoke some deity, he may certainly do so. Indeed, it is the usual practice among those who frequent pagodas to learn their fate; but it is done for good measure and is really superfluous. Nevertheless, although we do not know their exact nature, the forces we bring into play must be treated with respect. Many people believe that they can become dangerous and even turn against us if they are not wisely invoked.

This would seem to prove that in its conception Chinese astrology is fairly close to the early systems of Sumerian and Chaldean astrology. However, it has nothing in common with the art of fortune-tellers who try to reveal what will happen to you. For one thing, a Chinese does not believe that his destiny is pre-ordained; for another, he does not think that his personal fate is important enough[7] for him to consult oracles on the subject. One must seek to know not what is going to happen but what is the advisable thing to do.

The eight signs or four pillars determining our horoscopes will always be the touchstone of all divination affecting us. They are in a way our personal biorhythms and help us to know what we are and should never be ignored, particularly on important occasions in our lives. But when a decision has to be made or something undertaken, they must be complemented by other methods such as reading day by day the imperial calendar which tells us the best times for action as well as those which are personally the most propitious.[8] The calendar is limited, however, to giving indications which are not regarded as binding.

When a more important matter arises, we turn to an appropriate form of divination; and that is why the two systems presented here are a logical complement to my previous study of horoscopes. Many methods are used and there are countless experts in this field. As evidence of this, in places like Hongkong and Singapore where they are still numerous, one has only to visit the crowded pagodas to see how many interpreters of the oracles there are. Even in The People's Republic of China I have seen experts giving consultations on street corners in several provincial cities.

The oldest method, attested by thousands of inscriptions from the fourteenth century BC, is the cracking by fire of tortoise shells or the shoulder blades of oxen;[9] but, apart from the fact that its principles are not clearly understood, it would be hardly practicable these days. The second oldest method, and one that is described in the classics, is the *Yi Jing*.[10] divination by the sixty-four hexagrams. But the *Yi Jing* is a difficult book and, apart from a few learned people, most have recourse to it only on very important occasions with the help of specialists who perform the rite of counting the sticks and interpreting the hexagrams. For the uninitiated the book is as hard to understand as a medical treatise would be for most of us.

Very different from the *Yi Jing*, although they share its spirit, are those methods which use coins[11] ('pennies'),[12] five or six at a time, to form divinatory numbers. They are the easiest methods to use and are therefore very popular. The alignment of five or six pennies, which can be heads or tails, gives a pentagramic or hexagramic number analagous to the numbers of the *Yi Jing* to which, in the case of those formed by six pennies, the interpretation explicitly refers: tails=broken line=even=*yin*; heads=continuous line=odd=*yang*. In the first part of this book we shall study the thirty-two divinatory numbers formed by five pennies or pentagrams; in the second, the sixty-four numbers formed by six pennies or hexagrams. Each of these two parts will be introduced separately and I shall confine myself here to explaining their common features.

The reader should not be put off by the simplistic appearance of the presentation of the oracles. They are based on rhymed verses similar to popular proverbs in the West from the days when we still had a collective memory. Though we may find them disconcerting, the allegories, symbols and fables contained in this book are widely known in China. They form part of that oral folklore which still exists there and which is an important element in the transmission of knowledge and tradition.[13]

I call these methods 'divinatory games'. This does not mean that they are played for amusement – although they may be done with a smile – but because they appeal to what we call chance. However, as the Chinese do not believe in predetermination the results are not regarded as definitive. Nevertheless, the divinatory game is a serious rite which should be treated with respect. The advice given in some manuals emphasises how important it is to put oneself in the right frame of mind: we should think intensely about the matter in question; we should wash our hands and then, having found a quiet spot, light several sticks of incense. In short, we must find the best means of concentrating our minds.[14]

The question to be posed should be precise and detailed; but it should not be direct or blunt nor asked with too selfish or egotistical an aim. One should not ask: 'Shall I win the pools?' or 'Shall I be happy at home?' but rather: 'Should I gamble on the pools?', 'Should I ask Miss So and So to marry me?' One looks for advice about a course of action and not to know the outcome. A question should not be repeated the same day, nor should more than three questions be asked.

Before consulting what may properly be called oracles, I remember seeing in the pagodas of Saigon or Singapore, for example, that the devotees often carried out a preliminary operation to assure themselves that it was an auspicious moment to ask a question or if there was a chance of a response.[15] The supplicant would kneel on the ground and take in both hands a short piece of bamboo cut in two along its length, or perhaps two pieces of wood in the shape of half a French bean. After a moment's reflection while he concentrated on his question and, at the same time, held in both hands the two pieces placed together against his forehead, he would then throw them down before him. If they both fell on their flat surfaces, the oracle ought not to be consulted. If they fell on their convex surfaces, the tenor of the question had to be changed. In order to get a useful response from the oracle, one piece had to land on its flat surface and the other on its convex surface. Scaled down models of these pieces are available for use at home; or one can equally well throw two coins. The foregoing underlines the importance in Chinese eyes of the divinatory act, particularly if it is carried out in a religious context.

The casting of Chinese coins ('pennies') is done in the same manner: place five (or six) pennies in both hands which are cupped together in the shape of a conchshell; then press the hands against the forehead and think deeply about the question to be asked; then open the hands and let the pennies fall on the table (or on the floor in a temple for example); then quickly line up the pennies. The first in position is the lowest figure of the divinatory number which, as in the *Yi Jing*, is read from the bottom upwards. To find the divinatory number a value is attributed to each penny: heads 1, tails 2. (For practical reasons I prefer this convention to the one more generally employed when three pennies are used to form the hexagrams of the *Yi Jing*, where heads counts as 3 and tails as 2.)

The response to the question asked is never direct; this is not the Chinese way any more than it was for the Delphic oracle. It resembles rather a mandala[16] for it forms a theme which should be used as a support for our thoughts. It promotes an atmosphere which should help us to see clearly. A suggestion is made to us if we know how to understand it, but the decision is still our own.

It must be emphasised again that the response should not be taken to have a general application, although the words may sometimes suggest it. It is to be understood only in the sense of the question asked and that alone.

PART I

The Thirty-Two Pentagrams or Divination with the Five Golden Pennies

This is the type of popular divination most commonly used, and is published in almost identical form in all the annual almanacs. The responses vary slightly but the general sense is consistent. I have chosen to reproduce here the most widely used text which contains eight responses for each divinatory number.

The number given by the casting of five pennies (tails = even; heads = odd) is equivalent to a diagram made up of five lines. For this reason I have called the number a pentagram in contrast with the hexagrams formed by six lines.

The figure five   Earth is *yin* and thus would seem to indicate an even value; but, by an inversion emphasised by Granet,[17] it is five which is the terrestrial number associated with the Centre and the Nadir. Five is the number of the four cardinal points plus the Centre, of the forces emanating from the earth, the five Agents and the five movements derived from them. All are well known to acupuncturists.[18]

The fact that the oracles given here are linked to Earth perhaps explains their somewhat concrete character. It seems that this sort of divination may be used primarily for daily activities and events, while the hexagrams are reserved for more important matters.

Reading of the oracle   The title and the poem belong to the aspect (which gives an auspicious or inauspicious value), the most important element of the response. They indicate the atmosphere and the significance of the mandala; and, with a little reflection, they should in most cases help you to make your decision in a lucid way. Among the eight auguries, one or another should indicate a more precise response to your question. It is emphasised once again that the oracle should not be understood as having a general application, but solely as a response to the question asked.

Note: The five little drawings illustrating each pentagram represent the old Chinese copper coins or 'tongzier'. The ideograms are on the heads side.

The invention of the method of divination with five coins is attributed to Zhuge Liang, the hero of the *Romance of the Three Kingdoms* and famous for his perspicacity and knowledge of the magic arts.

List of Pentagrams

1st	11111	The heavenly bodies	Shangshang
2nd	22221	Easy change	Shangping
3rd	22212	Indirect approach	Xiaping
4th	22122	Too easy	Xiaoping
5th	21222	On the furnace	Xiaxia
6th	12222	Seedtime and harvest	Pingping
7th	22211	Hope fulfilled	Shangshang
8th	22121	Future assured	Shangji
9th	12221	Secure peace	Zhongji
10th	21221	Do as you will	Zhongji
11th	12112	Calamities vanish	Daji
12th	21212	The pentagram brings advancement	Shangping
13th	12212	Obscurity	Xiaxiong
14th	21122	Calm	Xiazhong
15th	12122	Obstacles	Xiaxiong
16th	11222	Security assured	Zhongji
17th	22111	Joy comes	Zhongji
18th	21211	Preserve integrity	Zhongping
19th	12211	Indecision	Xiaxia
20th	21121	Abundant harvest	Zhongji
21st	12121	Honours gained	Ji
22nd	11221	Shining light	Ji
23rd	21112	Happiness and honour	Ji
24th	22112	Frostbitten	Xia
25th	11212	Illustrious position	Ji
26th	11122	Happiness abounding	Ji
27th	11112	Great peace	Ji
28th	12111	Insurmountable obstacle	Xiong
29th	11211	Opening	Ping
30th	21111	Distinguished eagle	Ji
31st	11121	Happiness at last	Ping
32nd	22222	Incalculable	Xiong

Table of Pentagrams

11111	1st	12111	28th	21111	30th	22111	17th
11112	27th	12112	11th	21112	23rd	22112	24th
11121	31st	12121	21st	21121	20th	22121	8th
11122	26th	12122	15th	21122	14th	22122	4th
11211	29th	12211	19th	21211	18th	22211	7th
11212	25th	12212	13th	21212	12th	22212	3rd
11221	22nd	12221	9th	21221	10th	22221	2nd
11222	16th	12222	6th	21222	5th	22222	32nd

Aspects of the Pentagrams (in descending order of luck)

上上	Shangshang:	1st, 7th	中平	Zhongping:	18th
上吉	Shangji:	8th	小平	Xiaoping:	4th
大吉	Daji:	11th	下平	Xiaping:	3rd
吉	Ji:	21st, 22nd, 23rd, 25th, 26th, 27th, 30th	下中	Xiazhong:	14th
中吉	Zhongji:	9th, 10th, 16th, 17th, 20th	下	Xia:	24th
上平	Shangping:	2nd, 12th	下下	Xiaxia:	5th, 19th
平	Ping:	29th, 31st	凶	Xiong:	28th, 32nd
平平	Pingping:	6th	下凶	Xiaxiong:	13th, 15th

11111

First Pentagram 'The heavenly bodies'

Aspect: Excellent

Poem
The multi-coloured Phoenix shows its augury,
The Unicorn alights on the capital.[19]
Every unhappiness is averted; and everywhere
A joyous atmosphere spontaneously bursts out.

Auguries
- An assured career.
- Success in examinations.
- Lawsuits will be won.
- Sure recovery from illness.
- Complete success in enterprises.
- The lost one will be found.
- Happy marriage.
- One hundred per cent prosperity in business.

22221

Second Pentagram 'Easy change'

Aspect: Above average

Poem
You must change your job and learn[20]
To adapt yourself to favourable circumstances.
As the carp clears the rapids of Longmen,
Common 'bones' will become immortal.[21]

Auguries
- A career without problems.
- Everything will be accomplished.
- Agreement will be reached in lawsuits.
- Illness is not serious.
- Eighty per cent financial success.
- Hope of return of missing persons.
- Total success in marriage.
- Achievement in business.

22212

Third Pentagram 'Indirect approach'

Aspect: Below average

Poem
You must bend with the wind and
In your projects lean on others.
If you meet a dynamic official,
Everything will be arranged as you desire.

Auguries
- An assured career.
- All enterprises will succeed.
- In a lawsuit look for agreement.
- Illnesses are not serious.
- Average luck in money matters.
- You will not find those you are looking for.
- There may be a marriage.
- Great success in business.

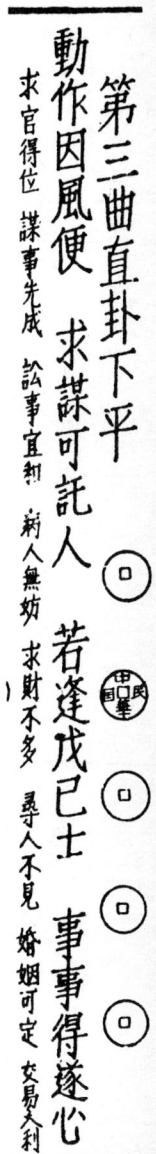

22122

Fourth Pentagram 'Too easy'

Aspect: Average

Poem
If you let your boat drift on the lake
Treasure will be hard to find.
You must make the best use of it
For happiness returns after the great heat ends.

Auguries
- Trade is quite profitable.
- Projects have a chance of success.
- Eighty per cent success in money matters.
- The sick are getting better.
- Favourable conclusion to a lawsuit.
- You have a chance of meeting those you are looking for.
- Marriages will be accomplished.
- Some business success.

21222

Fifth Pentagram 'On the furnace'

Aspect: Bad

Poem
This number being directed towards the South,[22]
Calamities and dangers are inevitable.
Lawsuits will not be won;
Disaster is imminent.

Auguries
- Your projects are dangerous.
- Unsuccessful journeys.
- You look for money in vain.
- Marriages will not be realised.
- Lawsuits will be lost.
- You will not find those for whom you are looking.
- No success in business.
- Travellers do not return.

12222

Sixth Pentagram 'Seedtime and harvest'

Aspect: Above average

Poem
Be content to live like an honest man.
Do not listen to the advice of the vulgar,
Be prudent in all things;
You will then know peace.

Auguries
- Your advice will not be listened to.
- Projects will not succeed.
- Journeys are a mistake.
- No success in examinations.
- Lawsuits unfavourable.
- The sick will not be cured.
- Difficult to succeed in marriage.
- You will look for money in vain.[23]

22211

Seventh Pentagram 'Hope fulfilled'

Aspect: Excellent

Poem
In a well-governed state the people know happiness
And the family gets progressively richer.
As your fortune improves in accordance with your desires,
Happiness and peace are also achieved.

Auguries
- Assured career.
- All enterprises succeed.
- Lawsuits are favourable.
- The sick will be cured.
- Total success of financial plans.
- Birth of a son with a great future.
- Successful marriage.
- Peace and happiness at home.

22121

Eighth Pentagram 'Future assured'

Aspect: Extremely good

Poem
Love of virtue receives the protection of heaven.
The whole family attracts a wind of happiness.
Many will help you with all their strength
To preserve joy and happiness.

Auguries
- Extremely brilliant career.
- All enterprises succeed.
- Lawsuits concluded according to your wishes.
- The sick are cured.
- One hundred per cent financial success.
- Marriage will be accomplished.
- Success in business.
- The family knows great happiness.

12221

Ninth Pentagram 'To secure peace'

Aspect: Good

Poem
For the moment this is the tree in Winter
Which withers without flowering.
Happily the Spring air comes
And the buds appear one by one.

Auguries
- Happy in lawsuits.
- The sick are out of danger.
- Money is easy to find.
- The traveller arrives.
- The home is happy.
- Marriage is a success.
- Business is concluded.
- A son will be born.

21221

Tenth Pentagram 'Do as you will'

Aspect: Good

Poem
When the breath of harmony comes,
Everything is alive again;
A light shower still falls.
All announce the return of Spring.

Auguries
- Assured career.
- Success in enterprises.
- Agreement can be reached in a lawsuit.
- The sick will be quickly cured.
- One hundred per cent financial success.
- Marriage will be achieved.
- Business is concluded.
- Peace in the home.

12112

Eleventh Pentagram 'Calamities vanish'

Aspect: Very good

Poem
As troubles pass, the door of happiness opens.
Unending joy comes to visit you.
If you can seize the auspicious hour,
You will win an unexpected fortune.

Auguries
- A very happy journey.
- Enterprise will succeed at last.
- Agreement is reached in a lawsuit.
- The sick are out of danger.
- Seventy per cent financial success.
- A son will be born.
- Marriage will be achieved.
- Business is concluded.

21212

Twelfth Pentagram   'The pentagram brings advancement'

Aspect: Favourable

Poem
Through success in the examinations,
A poor scholar rises in dignity.
Whoever gets this divinatory number
Can do all according to his desire.

Auguries
- Prosperous employment obtained.
- Enterprises will meet with a kind reception.
- Lawsuits completely successful.
- The sick are cured.
- Ninety per cent success in money matters.
- The traveller returns.
- The person from far away arrives.
- The journey brings prosperity.

12212

Thirteenth Pentagram 'Obscurity'

Aspect: The worst possible

Poem
When you look at the light of the moon at the bottom of the well,
You see only a shape without substance.
All your money disappears.
Prudence alone will bring you peace.

Auguries
- In your search nothing succeeds.
- Travel is unlucky.
- You search in vain for money.
- You do not find the one you look for.
- Your children are unsuccessful.
- Business is impossible.
- Peace in the home.
- Lawsuits are unsuccessful.[24]

21122

Fourteenth Pentagram 'Calm'

Aspect: Poor

Poem
Too many thoughts are confusing.
What you undertake will not succeed.
Patience alone can bring happiness.
Be resigned and you will avoid calamities.

Auguries
- No success in the examinations.
- Travel is without danger.
- Favourable lawsuits.
- Your enterprises will be difficult but successful.
- Little success for your financial plans.
- You will not find the one you look for.
- You will be married twice.
- Peace in the home.

第十四安靜卦下中

心思多不定 求謀未得成 忍耐方為福 守分免災星

功名不遂 出行不妨 訟事和 謀事必成 求財不利 尋人不見 婚姻二人 家宅早安

Fifteenth Pentagram 'Obstacles'

Aspect: The worst possible

Poem
The withered tree meets frost and snow,
The little boat the tempest.
The fearful heart without a hope
Can do nothing.

Auguries
- Your projects cannot succeed.
- Travel is not convenient.
- Money cannot be found.
- The absent one does not return.
- The birth will be that of a girl.
- The heart looks for peace.
- Many obstacles to marriage.
- Nothing is achieved in business.

11222

Sixteenth Pentagram 'Security assured'

Aspect: Good

Poem
The rising sun shines on the Eastern Sea.[25]
Light illuminates the Universe.
What luck that Harmony comes into play, for
Everything will be accomplished naturally.

Auguries
- Good chance of obtaining employment.
- Travel will give you satisfaction.
- All your projects succeed.
- The lawsuit will end satisfactorily.
- Seventy per cent luck in money matters.
- A son will be born.
- A marriage can be achieved.
- Misunderstandings disappear.

22111

Seventeenth Pentagram 'Joy comes'

Aspect: Good

Poem
All evils having vanished,
An air of happiness is born,
Just as a walker in the darkest night
Suddenly perceives the light of the moon.

Auguries
- The lawsuit is successfully concluded.
- The invalid is cured.
- By becoming an official, wealth is obtained.
- All projects can succeed.
- You will meet the one you are looking for.
- Journeys will be profitable.
- Eighty per cent success of financial plans.
- Marriage extremely happy.

第十七喜至卦中吉
眾惡皆消滅 端然福氣生
如人行暗夜 今巳得月明
訟得和 病人愈 八官得財 謀事可成 尋人見 出行求財 求財八分 姻婚大吉

21211

Eightenth Pentagram 'Preserve integrity'

Aspect: Average

Poem
Medicine must be taken to preserve the body.
You are not finished with lawsuits.
In everything you must follow tradition,
And thus be able naturally to create peace.

Auguries
- Peaceful journeys.
- Enterprises will be difficult at first.
- Disputes will not be dangerous.
- Lawsuits will be won.
- Sixty per cent financial success.
- A son will be born.
- Marriages start well.
- Business can be successful.

12211

Nineteenth Pentagram 'Indecision'

Aspect: Bad

Poem
This pentagram is the image of many illusions.
The word money remains in the shadows.
Gratitude changes to hate.
Human affairs make harmony impossible.

Auguries
- All projects fail.
- Journeys are calamitous.
- Lawsuits are hard to conclude satisfactorily.
- The one who is absent cannot be found.
- No success in finding money.
- Business fails.
- Misunderstandings in marriages.
- Illness gets worse.

Twentieth Pentagram 'Abundant harvest'

Aspect: Good

Poem
The roots are firm, branches and leaves flourish.
Trees are as numerous as they are lofty.
Enterprises will bring much money.
Orchids blossom in profusion.

Auguries
- A satisfactory promotion is obtained.
- Distant journeys succeed.
- All projects are realised.
- The one looked for will be found.
- The sick are out of danger.
- Eighty per cent success in money matters.
- Marriage achievable.
- Peace in the home.

12121

Twenty-First Pentagram 'Honours gained'

Aspect: Good

Poem
An honourable post is held with great renown.
Dragons and birds frolic with abandon.[26]
Wealth and treasure circulate.
Distant journeys are convenient.

Auguries
- All projects are realisable.
- Misunderstandings can be cleared up.
- Lawsuits are concluded successfully.
- The sick are cured.
- One hundred per cent success in money matters.
- A son will be born.
- A marriage will be realised in complete agreement.
- Business will be fruitful.

11221

Twenty-Second Pentagram 'Shining light'

Aspect: Good

Poem
The brilliant moon in the dark blue sky
Shines this night on feasting.
All families benefit from it,
And for ten thousand *li* it disperses clouds and vapours.[27]

Auguries
- The wished for promotion will be obtained.
- All projects will be realised.
- The one looked for will be found.
- Journeys will bring prosperity.
- Lawsuits will be ended by agreement.
- The traveller will return.
- Marriage will be achieved.
- Eighty per cent success in money matters.

21112

Twenty-Third Pentagram 'Happiness and honours'

Aspect: Good

Poem
Happiness and honour flourish.[28]
Prosperity is assured of progress.
Satisfaction in everything you do.
The scent of the orchid is wafted for ten thousand *li*.

Auguries
- Journeys will be auspicious.
- Full satisfaction in financial schemes.
- Absence of disputes.
- Lawsuits concluded favourably.
- Ninety per cent success in money matters.
- The traveller will return.
- Marriage is successful.
- Business accords with your wishes.

第二十三福祿卦吉

福祿得安康 榮華保進昌 所為皆遂意 千里共蘭香

出行大吉 謀財稱心 口舌不生 訟事和吉 求財九分 行人來 婚姻成 交易遂心

22112

Twenty-Fourth Pentagram 'Frostbitten'

Aspect: Bad

Poem
A skinny horse makes a long ride.
A starving man's journey is long.
Though confronted by dangerous obstacles,
There is no possibility of retreat.

Auguries
- No means of realising your wishes.
- A ruinous journey.
- In search of profit, capital is lost.
- In lawsuits arbitration is necessary.
- A birth will be that of a girl.
- Marriage will not be achieved.
- The invalid gets worse.
- At home troubles accumulate.

11212

Twenty-Fifth Pentagram 'Illustrious position'

Aspect: Good

Poem
Illustrious personages will help you.
A good star shines at your birth.
To him who shares in the evolution of the world
All the happinesses flow.[29]

Auguries
- You will obtain the Mandarin's seal.
- No more disputes.
- Lawsuits will end in agreement.
- Eighty per cent success in money matters.
- The traveller's return will be auspicious.
- Business prospers harmoniously.
- The sick are easily cured.
- A son will be born.

11122

Twenty-Sixth Pentagram 'Happiness abounding'

Aspect: Good

Poem
This pentagram interprets the whole Universe.
Those who aspire to riches will be filled with happiness.
Those who live far from home will return to their birthplace
And spontaneously break into a song of joy.

Auguries
- You will obtain the desired promotion.
- Journeys will bring you riches.
- The traveller will return.
- Lawsuits will bring large profits.
- Ninety per cent success in money matters.
- The man you are waiting for will surely arrive.
- Marriage will be successful.
- The sick are out of danger.

11112

Twenty-Seventh Pentagram 'Great peace'

Aspect: Good

Poem
The beneficent rain waters the seeded fields,
The harvest will be doubled without doubt.
Naturally the heart is joyous
When one can live in peace without anxiety.

Auguries
- Journeys will be auspicious.
- The absent will return.
- The lawsuit ends in agreement.
- Seventy per cent success in money matters.
- Success in examinations.
- Possibility of success in marriage.
- A son will be born.
- The invalid recovers his happiness.

12111

Twenty-Eighth Pentagram 'Insurmountable obstacles'

Aspect: Extremely bad

Poem
A traveller on a far off road,
The clouds darken and the sun goes down behind the mountains;
The fearful heart knows not whom to trust.
To advance or to retreat are equally difficult.

Auguries
- The search for employment will not succeed.
- Journeys should be avoided.
- In looking for profit you will lose your capital.
- The traveller does not return.
- Lawsuits are useless.
- Avoid marriage.
- No enterprise is successful.
- Bad outlook for the sick.

11211

Twenty-Ninth Pentagram 'Opening'

Aspect: Fair

Poem
The pearl leaves the shell.
Jade shines within the rock.
Money coming in is a sign of abundance.
Difficulties will not become calamities.

Auguries
- Average success in your career.
- Peaceful journeys.
- The traveller returns without trouble.
- In lawsuits it would be better to come to an agreement.
- Sixty per cent success in money matters.
- Possibility of success in marriage.
- The sick will find peace.
- Business difficult to start with.

21111

Thirtieth Pentagram 'Distinguished eagle'

Aspect: Good

Poem
The celestial army suppresses the bandits
And returns in triumph with banners flying.
Glorious actions bring promotion
Whose fame reflects on all the family.

Auguries
- Journeys very favourable.
- The traveller returns.
- Advantageous lawsuits.
- Sixty per cent success in money matters.
- Marriage will be achieved.
- A son will be born.
- Business is satisfactory.
- Projects and enterprises will do well.

11121

Thirty-First Pentagram 'Happiness at last'

Aspect: Fair

Poem
One marches with snow shoes over the frozen earth
And one can cross a dangerous bridge.
After braving peril after peril,
The colours of Spring bloom again.

Auguries
- Little success in the examinations.
- Peaceful journeys.
- The traveller returns without difficulty.
- Lawsuits in your favour.
- Fifty per cent success in money matters.
- You will not find the one you are looking for.
- Your aims will not be realised.
- A birth will be that of a girl.

22222

Thirty-Second Pentagram 'Incalculable'

Aspect: Extremely bad

Poem
Pieces of precious metal are buried in the dust,
Fine jade is stuck in the mud.
When once they reappear,
Only then will their splendour shine.

Auguries
- Hard to keep your job.
- Journeys will bring no profit.
- The traveller is sick.
- The lawsuit is unsuccessful.
- No success in money matters.
- The invalid gets worse.
- Marriage is disastrous.
- No aim is achieved.

PART II

The Sixty-Four Hexagrams or Divination with the Six Golden Pennies[30]

By the same inversion as explained in the introduction to the Thirty-Two Pentagrams whereby five is the terrestrial number, Earth being *yin* would normally be 'even', so Heaven being *yang* would indicate 'odd'. However, there are six energies which emanate from Heaven, three of them being *yang* and three *yin*. (Incidentally the practice of acupuncture is based on the six energies.)[31]

Less frequently used than the five pennies, divination with six is in fact a popular version of the *Yi Jing* to which it refers explicitly. Its answers are better adapted to the popular imagination than the symbols of the *Yi Jing* which, perhaps, is more suitable for scholars. However, for those who possess a copy of the *Yi Jing*, the tables in this book facilitate an instructive comparison between the two methods for the interpretation is quite difficult. In this type of divination the responses are less obvious than those of the pentagrams, demand a greater effort of concentration and, as such, are closer to the mandala. For those who use both systems, consulting the hexagrams seems to be reserved for more important matters.

The response The three elements of the response – symbol, poem, auguries – based as in the pentagrams on rhymed verses, are not so clearly separated as in the five coin system. The themes are jumbled together and sometimes no response may be apparent. Clearly it is principally the emotional tone, the atmosphere conveyed, which suggests the decision you should take. The answers sometimes make rather surprising associations: thus when illness and a quarrel are linked, both in Chinese eyes manifesting a disorder; or marriage and business which are both concerned with human relationships.

The Apologues (allegorical stories) are even more disconcerting for Westerners: they refer to a view of history made popular by storytellers and by the theatre and are known to everyone in China. The stories illustrate the designs on the corner of each page and expressly indicate that the hero of the tale has drawn the hexagram, though I have not thought it useful to mention the fact every time. Despite this the link is not always evident and the example does not always appear very convincing to us. Compared with those of the *Yi Jing* the conclusions are more concrete. *The Book of Changes* gives moral counsel rather than practical advice. Here again, in spite of the importance of the atmosphere, the answer should not be taken to have a wider meaning than is applicable to the question asked.

Note The coins illustrated on each page are rather modern! The two crossed flags indicate heads, while the ideograms (unlike the coins shown in the preceding part of this book) are tails.

List of Hexagrams

The numbers of the hexagrams in the *Yi Jing* are shown in brackets.

111111	1st (1)	121111	48th (13)	211111	2nd (44)	221111	3rd (33)
111112	54th (43)	121112	13th (49)	211112	31st (28)	221112	60th (31)
111121	8th (14)	121121	41st (30)	211121	43rd (50)	221121	42nd (56)
111122	53rd (34)	121122	14th (55)	211122	28th (32)	221122	63rd (62)
111211	34th (9)	121211	35th (37)	211211	33rd (57)	221211	24th (53)
111212	55th (5)	121212	12th (63)	211212	30th (48)	221212	61st (39)
111221	19th (26)	121221	18th (22)	211221	40th (18)	221221	17th (52)
111222	52nd (11)	121222	15th (36)	211222	29th (46)	221222	62nd (15)
112111	22nd (10)	122111	37th (25)	212111	47th (6)	222111	4th (12)
112112	57th (58)	122112	32nd (17)	212112	58th (47)	222112	59th (45)
112121	21st (38)	122121	38th (21)	212121	44th (64)	222121	7th (35)
112122	64th (54)	122122	25th (51)	212122	27th (40)	222122	26th (16)
112211	23rd (61)	122211	36th (42)	212211	46th (59)	222211	5th (20)
112212	10th (60)	122212	11th (3)	212212	9th (29)	222212	56th (8)
112221	20th (41)	122221	39th (27)	212221	45th (4)	222221	6th (23)
112222	51st (19)	122222	50th (24)	212222	16th (7)	222222	49th (2)

Concordance between the numbers of the Hexagrams in the *Heavenly Pennies* and those of the *Yi Jing* (Book of Changes).

Heavenly Pennies	Identification	Correspondence with the Yi Jing	
1st Hexagram	111111	Qian	No. 1
2nd Hexagram	211111	Gu	No. 44
3rd Hexagram	221111	Dun	No. 33
4th Hexagram	222111	Pi	No. 12
5th Hexagram	222211	Guan	No. 20
6th Hexagram	222221	Bo	No. 23
7th Hexagram	222121	Jin	No. 35
8th Hexagram	111121	Da you	No. 14
9th Hexagram	212212	Kan	No. 29
10th Hexagram	112212	Jie	No. 60
11th Hexagram	122212	Zhun	No. 3
12th Hexagram	121212	Ji ji	No. 63
13th Hexagram	121112	Ge	No. 49
14th Hexagram	121122	Feng	No. 55
15th Hexagram	121222	Ming yi	No. 36
16th Hexagram	212222	Shi	No. 7
17th Hexagram	221221	Gen	No. 52
18th Hexagram	121221	Pi	No. 22
19th Hexagram	111221	Da chu	No. 26
20th Hexagram	112221	Sun	No. 41
21st Hexagram	112121	Kui	No. 38
22nd Hexagram	112111	Lü	No. 10
23rd Hexagram	112211	Zhong fu	No. 61
24th Hexagram	221211	Jian	No. 53
25th Hexagram	122122	Zhen	No. 51
26th Hexagram	222122	Yu	No. 16
27th Hexagram	212122	Xie	No. 40
28th Hexagram	211122	Heng	No. 32
29th Hexagram	211222	Sheng	No. 46
30th Hexagram	211212	Jing	No. 48
31st Hexagram	211112	Da guo	No. 28
32nd Hexagram	122112	Sui	No. 17
33rd Hexagram	211211	Dun	No. 57
34th Hexagram	111211	Xiao shu	No. 9
35th Hexagram	121211	Jia ren	No. 37
36th Hexagram	122211	Yi	No. 42
37th Hexagram	122111	Wu wang	No. 25
38th Hexagram	122121	Shi he	No. 21
39th Hexagram	122221	Yi	No. 27

Heavenly Pennies	Identification	Correspondence with the Yi Jing	
40th Hexagram	211221	Gu	No. 18
41st Hexagram	121121	Li	No. 30
42nd Hexagram	221121	Lü	No. 56
43rd Hexagram	211121	Ding	No. 50
44th Hexagram	212121	Wei ji	No. 64
45th Hexagram	212221	Meng	No. 4
46th Hexagram	212211	Huan	No. 59
47th Hexagram	212111	Song	No. 6
48th Hexagram	121111	Tong ren	No. 13
49th Hexagram	222222	Kun	No. 2
50th Hexagram	122222	Fu	No. 24
51st Hexagram	112222	Lin	No. 19
52nd Hexagram	111222	Tai	No. 11
53rd Hexagram	111122	Da zhuang	No. 34
54th Hexagram	111112	Guai	No. 43
55th Hexagram	111212	Xu	No. 5
56th Hexagram	222212	Bi	No. 8
57th Hexagram	112112	Dui	No. 58
58th Hexagram	212112	Kun	No. 47
59th Hexagram	222112	Cui	No. 45
60th Hexagram	221112	Xian	No. 31
61st Hexagram	221212	Jian	No. 39
62nd Hexagram	221222	Qian	No. 15
63rd Hexagram	221122	Xiao guo	No. 62
64th Hexagram	112122	Gui mei	No. 54

111111

First Hexagram 'The imprisoned Dragon has found water again'

(*Note:* Water is the Dragon's natural element. After trying hard, patience is rewarded.)

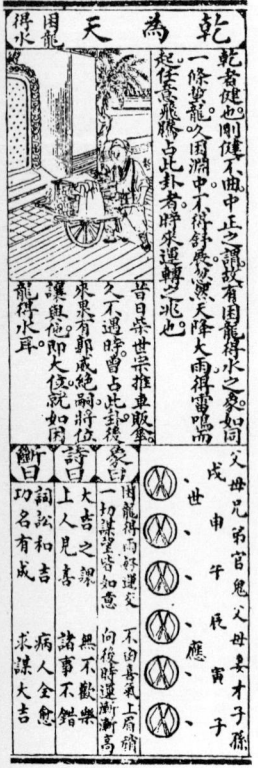

Symbol
Luck turns for the imprisoned Dragon;
Joy is reflected in his face.
All projects will be accomplished according to his wishes
And in the future his fortune can only grow.

Poem
This is the lesson of happiness:
All is joy.
Everyone is happy
And everything turns out well.

Auguries
All lawsuits are won.
Brilliant career.
The invalid is cured.
Nothing is difficult.

Apologue
Chai Shizong was no more than a travelling pedlar. Having drawn this hexagram, he had faith in his destiny and after many ups and downs he became the first emperor of the Song dynasty (AD 960).

Yi Jing 1st Hexagram *Qian* 'The Creative principle'
Trigrams Lower and upper: 'Heaven'

211111

Second Hexagram 'To meet a friend far from home'

Symbol
What joy to meet a friend when one is far from home.
From this fortune increases more and more.
Henceforth all will go well
And there is no need to worry about the future.

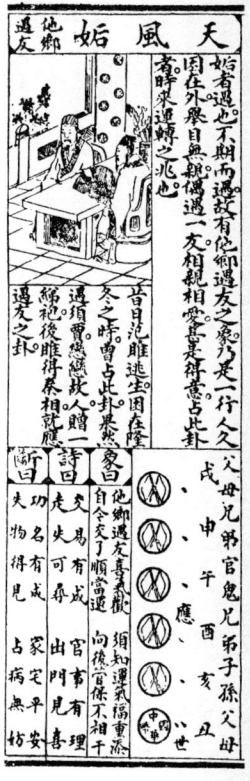

Poem
Business is entirely successful;
Litigation is satisfactorily concluded.
That which was lost is found;
Happiness appears on the threshold of the house.

Auguries
Success in examinations.
Lawsuit won.
One finds what one is looking for.
Illness is not dangerous.

Apologue
One winter a poor scholar, Fan Sui, met a true friend who offered him a silk padded robe. This auspicious gift presaged a new career and he became the prime minister of the famous emperor Qin Shihuang (*c.* 250 BC).

Yi Jing   44th Hexagram *Gu* 'Contact'
Trigrams   Lower: 'Wind'
             Upper: 'Heaven'
This hexagram signifies that after some difficulty everything will succeed.

221111

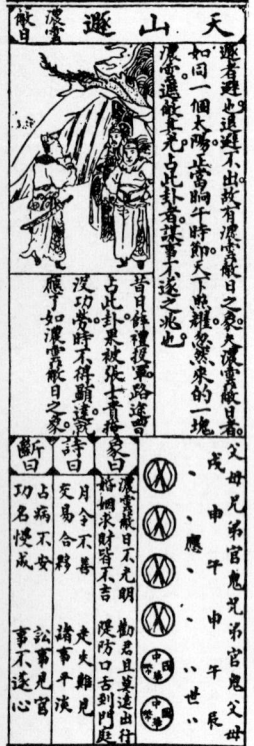

Third Hexagram 'Clouds hide the sun'

Symbol
Thick clouds hide the sun and not a gleam in sight.
Avoid going far from home.
Marriage and wealth will not come,
And your words may get you into trouble.

Poem
The whole month is bad
And what you seek cannot be found.
In business nothing comes from a co-operative venture.

Auguries
Worrying illness.
Unsuccessful lawsuit.
Career moves more slowly.
Nothing goes as one would like.

Apologue
General Xue Li of the Tang dynasty (seventh century AD) never succeeded in getting promotion, for his superior, being an upstart, failed to report his achievements.

(*Note:* The meaning of the oracle is that for the time being something or someone gets in the way, but this is perhaps only momentary.)

Yi Jing 33rd Hexagram *Dun* 'Retreat'
Trigrams Lower: 'Mountain'
            Upper: 'Heaven'
It is better to make a strategic withdrawal than to persevere when fate is against you.

222111

Fourth Hexagram 'The tiger falls in a pit'

Symbol
When the tiger falls in the pit, there is nothing he can do;
He can neither advance nor retreat.
None of his projects can be accomplished.
And he is the prisoner of both his maladies and his enemies.

Poem
The search is vain and business uncertain.
Marriage is difficult; hasty decisions should be avoided.

Auguries
Money is lacking.
Those you count on remain invisible.
Travel is inadvisable.
Things are only done tardily.

Apologue
Lin Chong (one of the heroes of *The Water Margin*) is accused of stealing a valuable sword and is exiled.

(*Note:* In Chinese eyes the oracle is not entirely unfavourable because the difficulty is only temporary.)

Yi Jing 12th Hexagram *Pi* 'Stagnation'
Trigrams Lower: 'Earth'
            Upper: 'Heaven'
Too great an equilibrium between Earth and Heaven results in stagnation; but this cannot be permanent.

222211

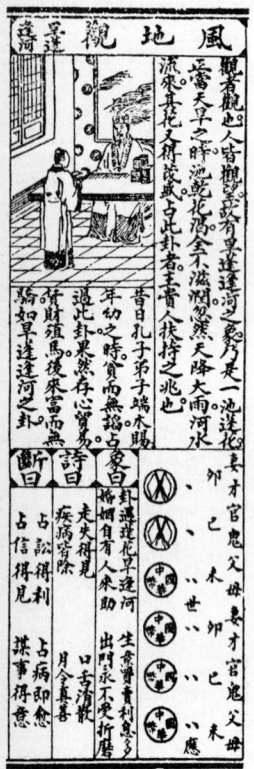

Fifth Hexagram 'Beneficent rain on parched earth'

Symbol
The parched lotus blooms after beneficent rain.
In business your interests are fruitful.
You will obtain support in marriage.
You will be well received wherever you may travel.

Poem
You will find what you are looking for.
Misunderstandings disappear.
Illnesses will be cured.
The whole month will be prosperous.

Auguries
Lawsuits will be won.
Illnesses easy to cure.
The expected letter will arrive.
All will happen as you wish.

Apologue
As a result of this oracle, Duan mu Ci (a disciple of Confucius) decided to go into business and became immensely rich.

Yi Jing   20th Hexagram *Guan* 'Looking down'
Trigrams   Lower: 'Earth'
             Upper: 'Wind'

222221

Sixth Hexagram 'The eagle and the dove live in the same wood'

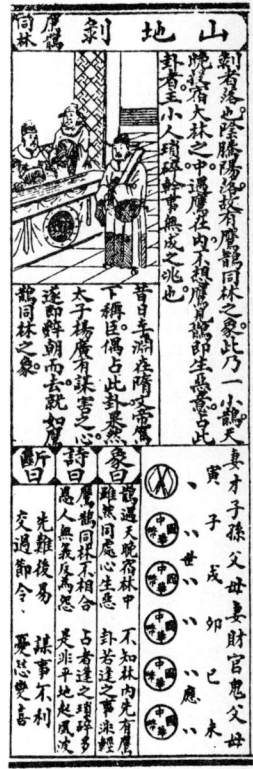

Symbol
At night time the dove nests in the wood,
But it is unaware that the eagle is perched in the same place.
And the eagle has an evil heart.
Whoever draws this hexagram should be careful.

Poem
Eagle and dove can never get on together,
And this is a warning of troubles to come.
In return for a service, gratitude becomes hate,
And the tempest will be born in a calm place.

Auguries
Difficulties will be overcome slowly.
Projects will barely succeed.
Wait for the bad times to pass
And grief will be transformed into joy.

Apologue
Threatened with death in consequence of the jealousy which he aroused in the son of his protector, Li Yuan resigned and had to depart. However, he finally ended up as the first emperor of the Tang dynasty (AD 618).

(*Note:* The apologue proves that although this hexagram counsels prudence it is only temporarily unfavourable.)

Yi Jing　23rd Hexagram *Bo* 'Peeling off'
Trigrams　Lower: 'Earth'
　　　　　　Upper: 'Mountain'
This hexagram signifies that one should get rid of obstacles.

222121

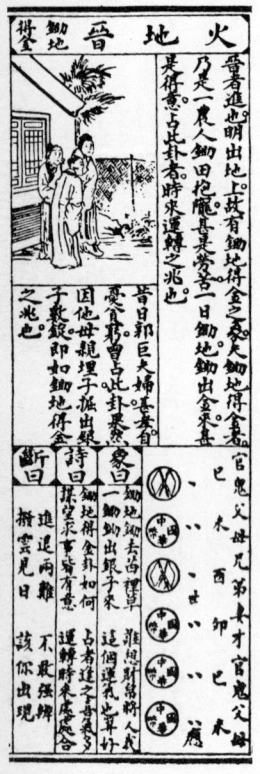

Seventh Hexagram 'Find money by digging in the ground'

Symbol
Weeding is tedious work
For him who expects to find gold;
But when treasure appears bit by bit,
What extraordinary luck.

Poem
What exceptional luck to find treasure by turning the sod.
Everything will then smile on you and a fortunate wind will blow everywhere.

Auguries
If you do not know whether to advance or retreat,
Take your time in making a decision.
When the clouds blow away, the sun appears:
Your hour has arrived.

Apologue
A poor honest couple find treasure while they are burying their son.

(*Note:* The text of this hexagram is odd to say the least, but it simply means that even great unhappiness can have a beneficent outcome.)

Yi Jing 35th Hexagram *Jin* 'Progress'
Trigrams Lower: 'Earth'
            Upper: 'Fire'

111121

Eighth Hexagram 'Catch sparrows when cutting down the tree'

Symbol
To catch sparrows in their nest, do not hesitate to cut down a tree;
And thus make sure of success.
All misunderstandings will automatically disappear.
No effort is needed to make sure of partners in marriage or business.
Those you look for are not far away.

Poem
The recipient of this hexagram has great luck.
If he can take drastic measures, he will surely achieve his aim,
While the rest will get nowhere.

Auguries
Do not be satisfied with second best, but make sure of the means of success.
If you are after honour and riches, you will find them automatically.

Apologue
Hu Pixian, ordered to arrest a wicked governor, sought first to take possession of his seal.*

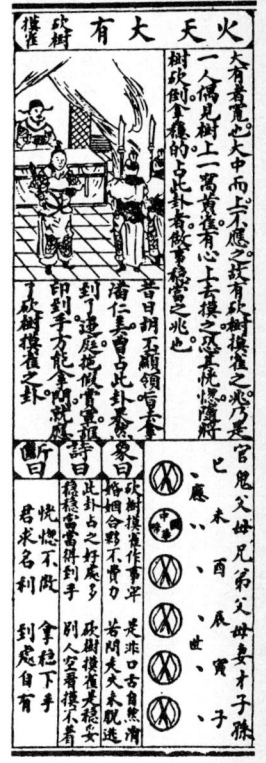

* Without his seal a mandarin had no authority, for his authority derived from the seal conferred on him by the emperor.

Yi Jing 14th Hexagram *Da you* 'Great possessions'
Trigrams   Lower: 'Heaven'
             Upper: 'Fire'

212212

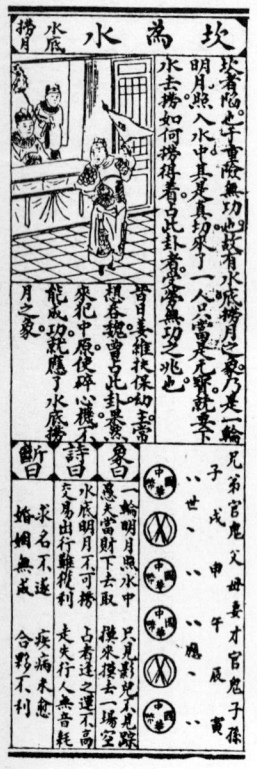

Ninth Hexagram 'Look for the moon under the water'

Symbol
Moonlight is reflected in the water,
But only the image, not the reality, is seen.
The drunken sot takes it for true riches,
But do what he can, all is in vain.

Poem
One tries in vain to grasp the moon's reflection in the water.
He who draws this hexagram is given little luck:
He profits little from his relationships
And he will not find those he is looking for.

Auguries
Success will not be obtained.
Sickness will not be cured.
No success in marriage.
No good partners in business.

Apologue
Jiang Wei (hero of *The Romance of the Three Kingdoms*) tried in vain to conquer the land of Wei from Cao Cao but he died before achieving his object.

(*Note:* Mirages should be mistrusted.)

Yi Jing   29th Hexagram *Kan* 'The Abyss'
Trigrams   Lower and Upper: 'Water'

112212

Tenth Hexagram 'Kill the General and canonise his soul'

Symbol
Luck changes and joy comes.
The Celestial General canonises the dead generals;
In spite of their unhappiness,
The spirits of the generals after their death are no longer malignant.

Poem
The support of ancestors gives certainty to those who seek fortunes.
Business will prosper and there will be no more sickness or disputes.

Auguries
The month will be good.
Your reputation grows.
Good news of absent ones.
No worries in lawsuits.

Apologue
Han Xin (hero of the *Three Kingdoms*) had a difficult start in life; but after receiving this oracle, he was presented to the emperor and became a high dignitary.

(*Note:* The general meaning of this hexagram is that misery can be transformed into happiness.)

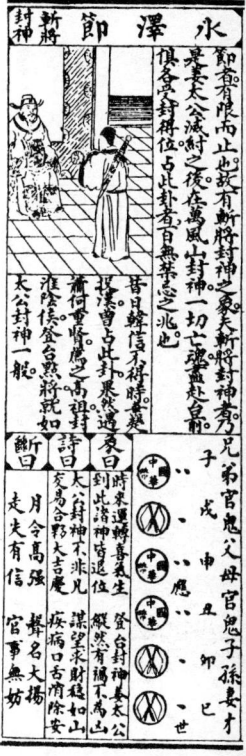

Yi Jing   60th Hexagram *Jie* 'Restraint'
Trigrams   Lower: 'Lake'
              Upper: 'Water'

122212

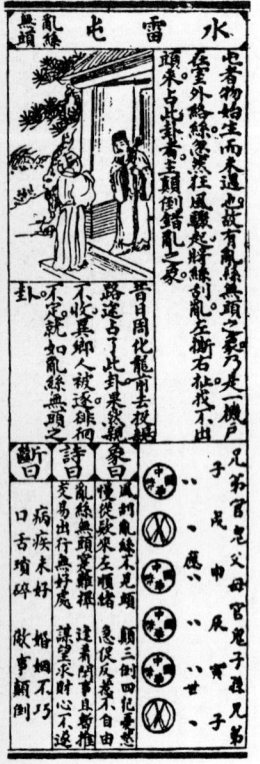

Eleventh Hexagram 'Tangled hair which cannot be disentangled'

Symbol
When the wind blows on tangled thread the end cannot be found.
Certainly such disorder is saddening.
You must take your time to sort it out.
You will gain nothing by hurrying.

Poem
The end of a tangled ball of wool cannot be found:
In such a case it would be better to put it off until later.
Nothing succeeds in business or on journeys.
The gains will not be satisfying.

Auguries
Illness will not be cured.
Marriage will not be happy.
Disputes will cause trouble.
Business is topsy-turvy.

Apologue
Zhou Hualong, having come to take refuge in his village, sees all the gates shutting before him. Everything goes round in circles like a tangled ball of wool.

Yi Jing   3rd Hexagram *Zhun* 'Difficulty'
Trigrams   Lower: 'Thunder'
             Upper: 'Water'

121212

Twelfth Hexagram 'First on the list in the examinations'

Symbol
He who has taken first place in the examinations
Surely did not work in vain when he was young.
To find this hexagram is cause for congratulations
For it signifies that projects and hopes will be realised.

Poem
Having come first in the examinations, you shine with happiness.
You will spread your joy about you everywhere.
Today's good fortune augurs continued promotion.

Auguries
Everything is perfect this month.
You will find those you are looking for.
Missing persons return.
All misunderstandings evaporate.

Apologue
The poet Sima Xiangru (under the Han dynasty, second century BC) worked during his youth with courage and perseverance and was able in the end to realise his ambitions.

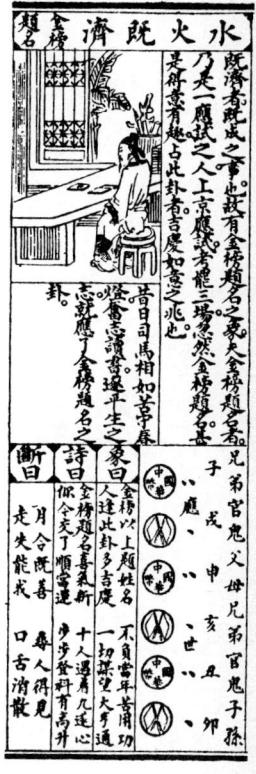

Yi Jing 63rd Hexagram *Ji ji* 'After completion'
Trigrams Lower: 'Fire'
Upper: 'Water'
Beware, success is not without its dangers!

121112

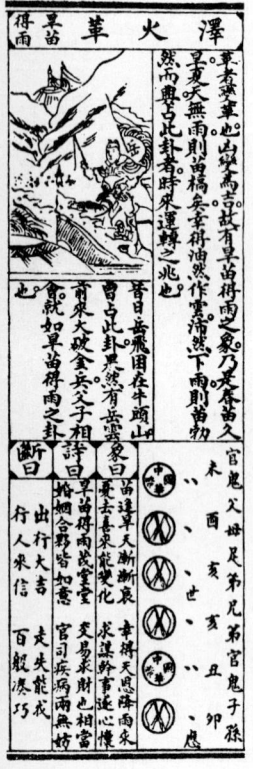

Thirteenth Hexagram 'Parched earth has received rain'

Symbol
Drought has insidiously withered the shoots;
But now Heaven makes beneficent rain to fall.
When melancholy disappears, joy comes.
In enterprises and business, everything responds to our desires.

Poem
The parched plants expand under the rain.
In the search for wealth everything succeeds.
In the household as in business, partners are satisfactory.
There is nothing to fear from lawsuits or illness.

Auguries
Journeys are very happy.
You will find what you are looking for.
Letters from people far away.
All turns out according to your wishes.

Apologue
General Yue Fei (1103–41: end of Song dynasty), surrounded on 'Oxhead' mountain, is rescued by his son.

Yi Jing   49th Hexagram *Ge* 'Revolution'
Trigrams   Lower: 'Fire'
             Upper: 'Lake'

121122

Fourteenth Hexagram 'An antique mirror recovers its brightness'

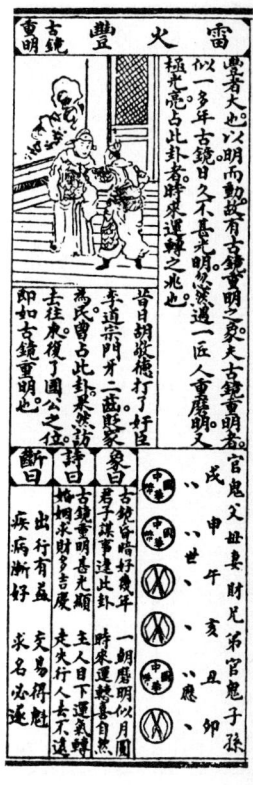

Symbol
An antique mirror, tarnished for years,
Recovers one day its brightness and becomes as brilliant as the moon.
He who draws this hexagram
Can only congratulate himself that happiness has at last come to him.

Poem
When the antique mirror recovers its brightness,
Its owner sees a change of fortune.
Good luck in love and money matters.
Travellers are not far away.

Auguries
Profitable journeys.
Success in business.
Illnesses improve.
Your reputation grows.

Apologue
Hu Jingde, after being reduced to the most humble circumstances for many years, drew this hexagram, recovered the favour of his master and became a high dignitary.

Yi Jing 55th Hexagram *Feng* 'Abundance'
Trigrams   Lower: 'Fire'
           Upper: 'Thunder'

121222

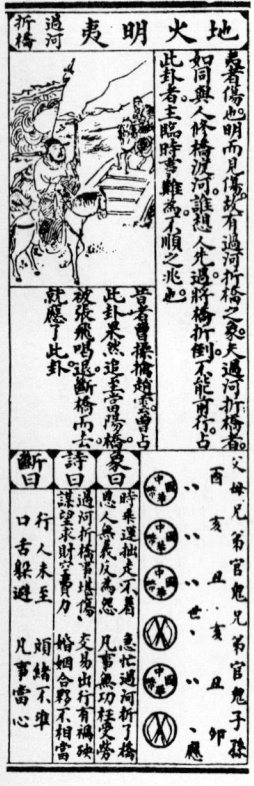

Fifteenth Hexagram 'Destroy the bridge after crossing'

Symbol
Under the malignant star, one knows not where to go.
It were better to cross the river quickly and destroy the bridge.
Gratitude turns to hate.
Whatever you do, all is in vain.

Poem
It is sad to destroy the bridge after crossing the river.
Business and journeys will be disastrous.
Attempts to enrich oneself are vain.
Neither partnership nor marriage is advisable.

Auguries
Travellers do not arrive.
Business does not go well.
Try to avoid quarrels.
Be prudent in everything.

Apologue
General Zhang Fei (hero of the *Three Kingdoms*) succeeded in preventing Cao Cao from capturing Zhao Yun, one of his rivals, only by burning the bridge.

Yi Jing 36th Hexagram *Ming yi* 'Darkening of the light'
Trigrams Lower: 'Fire'
            Upper: 'Earth'

212222

Sixteenth Hexagram 'Victory when the charger arrives'

Symbol
The general receives orders to undertake an expedition.
He mounts his fine charger and draws his bow.
At a hundred paces his arrow pierces a leaf of a weeping willow.
What a happy augury.

Poem
At the arrival of the victorious horse, joy is unconfined.
For fame and profit the opportunity is there.
No obstacles to partnerships or marriages.
Go peaceably about your business and on your travels.

Auguries
Illnesses improve greatly.
You will easily find those you are looking for.
Travellers will write.
All will go as you desire.

Apologue
Guan Gong (a celebrated general of the *Three Kingdoms* who became 'god of war') while dining with one of his friends, absented himself for a moment in order to kill the opposing general Hua Xiong in the service of Cao Cao. On his return, the wine in his cup was still warm.

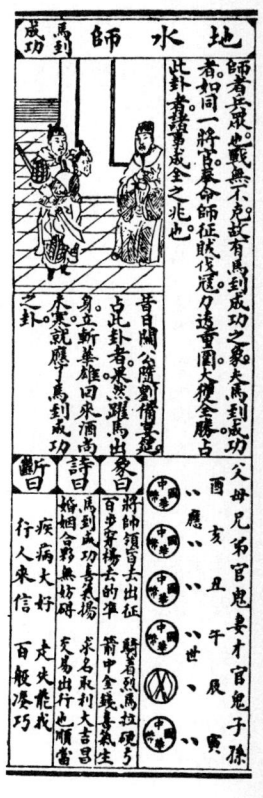

Yi Jing　　7th Hexagram *Shi* 'The army'
Trigrams　　Lower: 'Water'
　　　　　　Upper: 'Earth'

221221

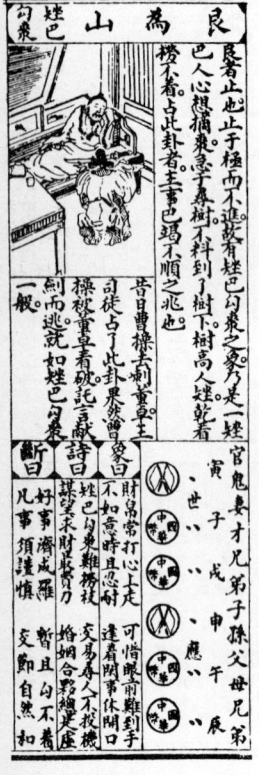

Seventeenth Hexagram 'The dwarf tries to gather jujubes'

Symbol
The desire for riches often tantalises your heart.
Unhappily they are just out of reach.
If your wishes cannot be satisfied, be patient
And be silent in matters which do not concern you.

Poem
The dwarf tries to gather jujubes although the branches are out of reach.
Profit and honours are hard to get.
To earn money requires a special effort.
Marriages and partnerships will fail.

Auguries
To succeed in business becomes more and more difficult.
Everything is out of reach.
Be cautious in everything.
Later all will go better.

Apologue
Dong Zhuo (hero of the *Three Kingdoms*) perceives that Cao Cao intends to murder him although he claims that he wished only to offer him his sword.

Yi Jing   52nd Hexagram *Gen* 'Desisting'
Trigrams   Lower and Upper: 'Mountain'

121221

Eighteenth Hexagram 'Happiness comes to your door'

Symbol
The time has come for fortune to smile on you.
The beautiful girl is wooed by a noble suitor.
Music resounds in a climate of joy.
The star of happiness shines on him who draws this horoscope.

Poem
The spirit of happiness is in your luck;
Even calamity will be transformed into joy.
Marriages and relationships will improve.
In business profits increase day by day.

Auguries
Happy journeys.
No obstacles in business.
Something lost will be found.
The whole month is favourable.

Apologue
Nan Rong, a disciple of Confucius, was so highly thought of by the Master that he gave him his niece in marriage.

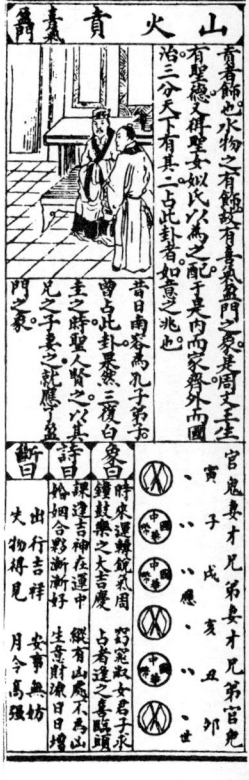

Yi Jing   22nd Hexagram *Pi* 'Elegance'
Trigrams   Lower: 'Fire'
             Upper: 'Mountain'

111221

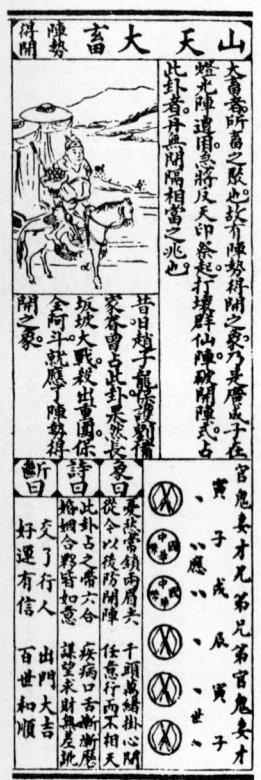

Nineteenth Hexagram 'Find the weak point'

Symbol
Anxieties make one frown,
A thousand cares grip the heart.
From now on take care to attack the weakest point
And you can go anywhere without fear.

Poem
Whoever draws this hexagram can ease sickness and pacify the quarrelsome.
Marriage and partnerships will be satisfactory.
Ambition will be realised.

Auguries
People far away return.
Journeys bring happiness.
News of good luck.
Good understanding in the family.

Apologue
General Zhao Zilong (*Romance of the Three Kingdoms*) succeeded in saving the little prince, son of the pretender, whom Cao Cao wanted to kill, by attacking the weakest point in Cao Cao's positions.

Yi Jing 26th Hexagram *Da chu* 'The great nourisher'
Trigrams Lower: 'Heaven'
Upper: 'Mountain'
The sage knows to nourish his virtue. The time is favourable for travel.

112221

Twentieth Hexagram 'To push a wheelbarrow off balance'

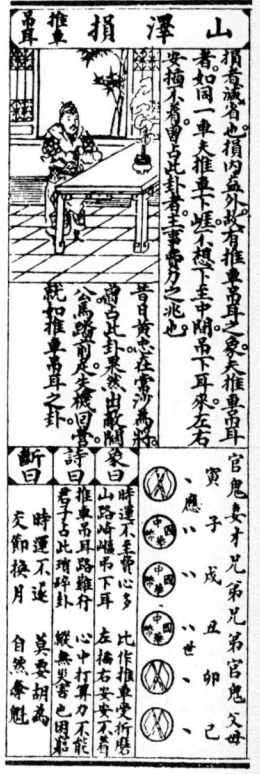

Symbol
When luck does not smile, it is futile to multiply your efforts.
It is like a wheelbarrow off balance when it is pushed on mountain tracks
Without being able to stop it from falling to the right or the left.

Poem
It is hard to push a wheelbarrow on a winding path
Whatever one does one lacks the strength.
Whoever is unlucky enough to draw this hexagram
May, perhaps, escape calamity but will not avoid difficulties.

Auguries
If luck does not smile on you, don't gamble.
Wait until the wheel of fortune turns.

Apologue
General Huang Zhong (*Romance of the Three Kingdoms*) wanted to fight with Guan Gong (see sixteenth Hexagram) but, his horse having strained a leg, he was forced to withdraw.

Yi Jing 41st Hexagram *Sun* 'Loss'
Trigrams Lower: 'Lake'
Upper: 'Mountain'
Blofeld considers this hexagram as rather favourable since the loss is only temporary.

112121

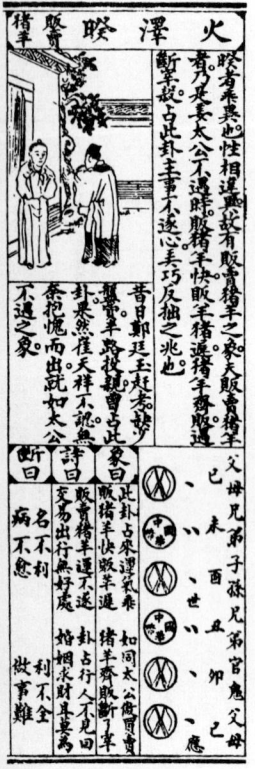

Twenty-First Hexagram 'On being reduced to selling pigs and goats'

Symbol
This hexagram is the bearer of misfortune,
As for the Prime Minister who had to sell some livestock before seeing his luck turn.
Whether the sale was profitable or not,
The animals were all sent to the butcher.

(*Note:* The trade of butcher or supplier of meat was always considered, particularly after the advent of Buddhism, to be especially degrading.)

Poem
Being reduced to such a trade is bad luck.
The far off person will not return.
Useless to try to do business far away.
Avoid marriages and do not count on getting rich.

Auguries
No success in your career.
No chance of wealth.
Illnesses are incurable.
There is difficulty in everything.

Apologue
Zheng Tingyu did not have enough money for the journey to the capital in order to take part in the examinations. He was turned away from every door on which he knocked.

Yi Jing 38th Hexagram *Kui* 'The estranged'
Trigrams   Lower: 'Lake'
             Upper: 'Fire'

112111

Twenty-Second Hexagram 'The Phoenix sings on Mount Qui'

Symbol
The phoenix alights on Mount Qui in the west.
He sings and causes sages and saints to be born.
Heaven commands Wen Wang to found his dynasty,
Thereby inaugurating eight hundred years of wealth and prosperity.

(Wen Wang was the father of the first sovereign of the Zhou dynasty 1121 BC.)

Poem
When the Phoenix sings on Mount Qui he is heard everywhere.
Whoever draws this hexagram will rejoice in the greatest happiness.
The long expected travellers will give their news.
Every enterprise will open to you the gates of the land of riches.

Auguries
Journeys will be advantageous.
Success in business is sure.
Illnesses will disappear.
Your enterprises will end happily.

Apologue
After drawing this hexagram Yan Song (*c.* AD 1522) became prime minister and brought prosperity to the state and peace to the people.

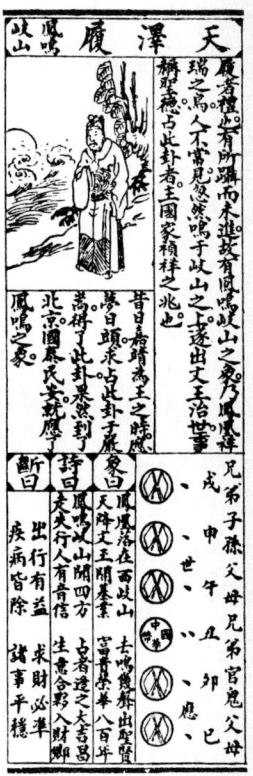

Yi Jing 10th Hexagram *Lü* 'Treading'
Trigrams Lower: 'Lake'
 Upper: 'Heaven'
Although favourable, this hexagram suggests that great prudence is required.

112211

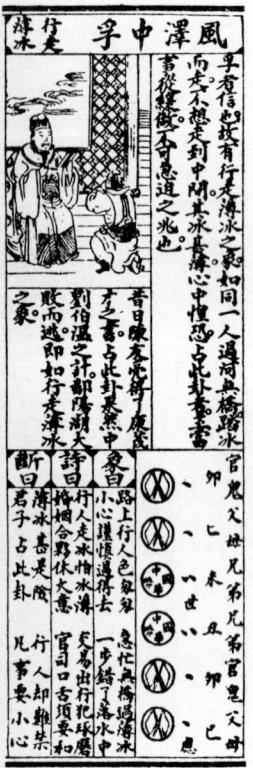

Twenty-Third Hexagram 'Walking on thin ice'

Symbol
The walker on the road is in a great hurry.
He wants to cross the frozen river where there is no bridge.
He walks with great care;
One false step and he will fall into the water.

Poem
The pedestrian who crosses the river should distrust the thin ice.
He should be extremely cautious in business and on journeys.
Pay close attention to your choice of partner in marriage or enterprises.
Avoid quarrels and lawsuits as much as possible.

Auguries
Thin ice is dangerous,
Although the pedestrian is obliged to cross over.
Whoever draws this hexagram should be careful in all things.

Apologue
Chen Youliang, a general of the Ming dynasty, unwisely engaged the enemy on lake Poyang and was defeated.

Yi Jing 61st Hexagram *Zhong fu* 'Inward confidence'
Trigrams Lower: 'Lake'
           Upper: 'Heaven'
Very differing interpretations of this hexagram. Both confidence and profound thought are necessary.

221211

Twenty-Fourth Hexagram 'The pretty bird leaves its cage'

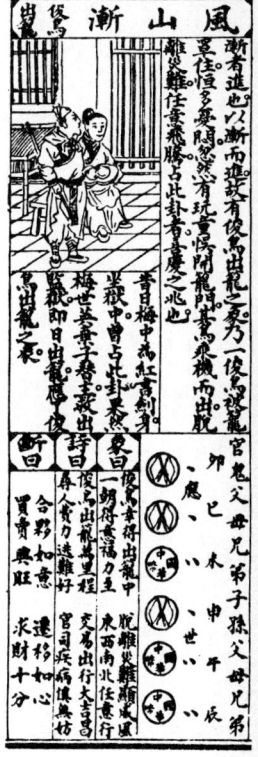

Symbol
By chance the pretty bird has left his cage.
In freeing himself from his difficulties he shows his glory.
When one morning this happiness comes to him,
He can fly as he pleases in all directions.

Poem
The pretty bird emerges to a brilliant future.
Success in business or on journeys can be his.
He will escape all miseries.
And has nothing to fear from lawsuits or illnesses.

Auguries
All relationships are satisfying.
Successful journeys.
Business prospers.
One hundred per cent profit.

Apologue
After having been imprisoned for a long time, Mei Zhong was saved by his servants and succeeded in making a brilliant career for himself.

Yi Jing 53rd Hexagram *Jian* 'Gradual progress'
Trigrams   Lower: 'Mountain'
             Upper: 'Wind'

122122

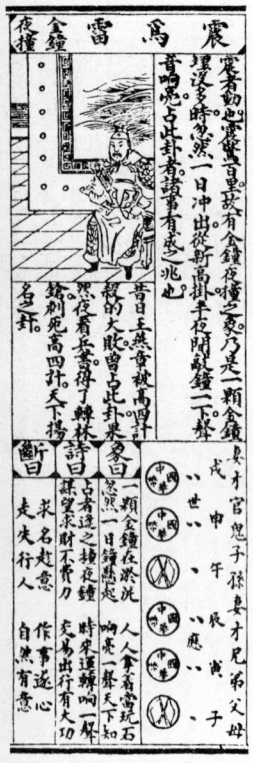

Twenty-Fifth Hexagram 'The golden clock strikes at night'

Symbol
If a golden clock falls in the mud,
Anyone can make a plaything of it.
On the day when it is hung up in an elevated place,
Its resonance is known throughout the world.

Poem
Whoever draws this hexagram sounds like the clock at night.
When the opportunity arrives, it is enough to strike a blow.
A career and wealth are found without difficulty.
Business and travel will bring great success.

Auguries
A career according to your desires.
Business fulfils your hopes.
Those far away return.
Everything responds to your wishes.

Apologue
General Wang Yanzhang had been defeated by Gao Siji. He then drew this hexagram and spent the whole night in studying a book on strategy which helped him to conquer and kill his rival and to become famous.

Yi Jing   51st Hexagram *Zhen* 'Thunder'
Trigrams   Lower and upper: 'Thunder'

222122

Twenty-Sixth Hexagram 'The Dragon takes his place'

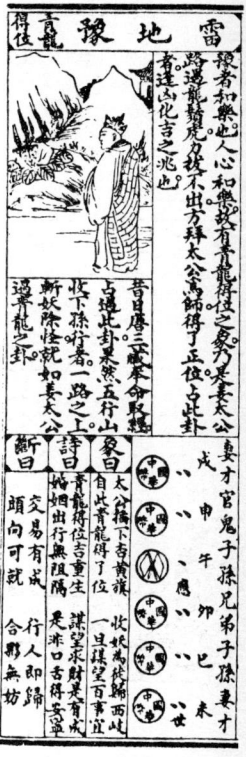

Symbol
The celestial marshal has raised the yellow standard
And has successfully taken back the evil spirits to Mount Qui in the West.
Henceforth the Dragon can take his place
And all projects can be accomplished without hindrance.

(*Note:* It seems that this allegory symbolises the victory of the East, life and light over the Spirits of the West, death and night, when the latter are returned to their own place. The yellow standard is an imperial symbol.)

Poem
The green Dragon occupies his place and happiness is born again.
Whoever looks for profit will have complete success.
No obstacle to marriage or journeys.
Controversies and quarrels compose themselves.

Auguries
Success in business.
The traveller returns.
The direction of your career is assured.
No difficulty in reaching agreement with third parties.

Apologue
The wandering monk San Zang who, after much travelling, brought the holy books of Buddhism to China, is the hero of the celebrated tale of his journey to the West, the Xiyouji. Although the monkey who accompanied him has largely eclipsed him in popularity, he remains the principal actor of the story in which he is held up as an example for his courage as much as his success.

Yi Jing 16th Hexagram *Yu* 'Repose'
Trigrams Lower: 'Earth'
Upper: 'Thunder'
Blofeld prefers 'repose' to 'enthusiasm' used by Wilhelm for it suggests rest after a success.

212122

Twenty-Seventh Hexagram 'Getting out of trouble'

Symbol
This month it looks as if one should climb over the walls,
For one thousand pitfalls and ten thousand miseries overwhelm us.
Suddenly someone turns up to save us.
He must be allowed to do it without fuss.

Poem
When you emerge from a period of adversity, your luck turns,
And you must take advantage of it to look for riches.
In business people will help you.
Fear neither quarrels nor illness.

Auguries
Great happiness at home.
The traveller soon returns.
All projects are accomplished and
Business is in marvellous shape.

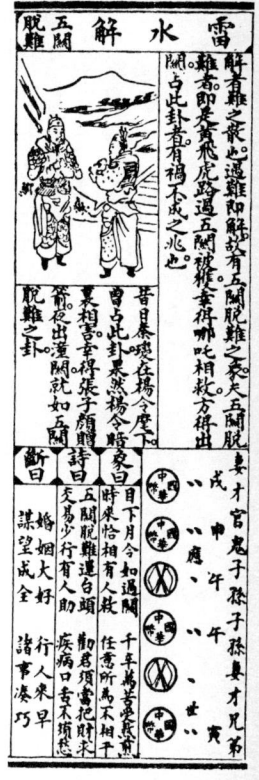

Apologue
Qin Qiong (Tang dynasty about the seventh century AD) was threatened with death by his superior Yang Lin. A friend helped him to escape during the night and to cross the pass through the Great Wall.

Yi Jing   40th Hexagram *Xie* 'Release'
Trigrams   Lower: 'Water'
             Upper: 'Thunder'
This hexagram implies that activity is required in the face of danger.

211122

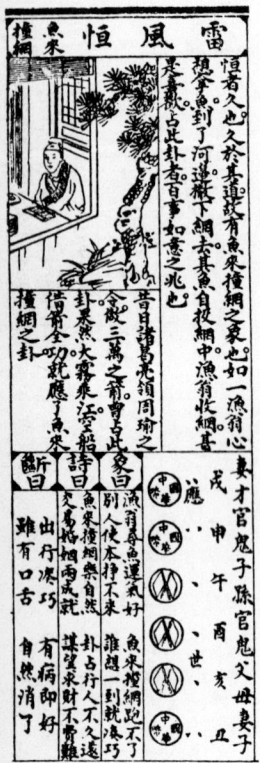

Twenty-Eighth Hexagram 'The fish swims into the net'

Symbol
What good luck for the happy fisherman!
There go the fish racing each other into his nets.
The other fishermen have taken practically nothing,
But he had hardly arrived before he succeeded.

Poem
The fish race into the nets with joy.
The traveller who draws this hexagram will soon return.
Both marriage and business go well.
Career and profits, everything is easy.

Auguries
Journeys are favourable.
Illness is cured.
Quarrels are quite easily settled.

Apologue
Zhuge Liang, a famous strategist in the era of the *Three Kingdoms*, succeeded one foggy night in 'borrowing' thirty thousand arrows from the enemy. During the night he sent some boats loaded with straw down the river in front of the enemy camp. As they passed they were riddled with arrows.

Yi Jing   32nd Hexagram *Heng* 'The long enduring'
Trigrams   Lower: 'Wind'
               Upper: 'Thunder'

211222

Twenty-Ninth Hexagram 'Dreaming of sunrise'

Symbol
The scholar who draws this hexagram is assured of a brilliant career.
Merchants will do exceptionally brilliant business.
Artisans will be sure to sell their products.
In the countryside the peasants will have an excellent harvest.

Poem
To dream of the sun rising in the sky brings a new atmosphere.
Missing persons and travellers will give their news.
Examinations and travels will match your hopes.
Illness and quarrels will vanish.

Auguries
You obtain the wealth you wanted.
All your projects are accomplished.
You will find the one you are looking for.
At home peace reigns.

Apologue
Kou Zhunshen, an obscure young magistrate, on arriving in the capital, unexpectedly obtains the post of Minister of Justice.

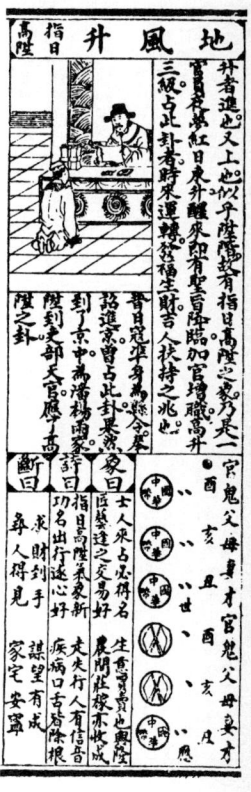

Yi Jing 46th Hexagram *Sheng* 'Promotion'
Trigrams   Lower: 'Wind'
            Upper: 'Earth'

211212

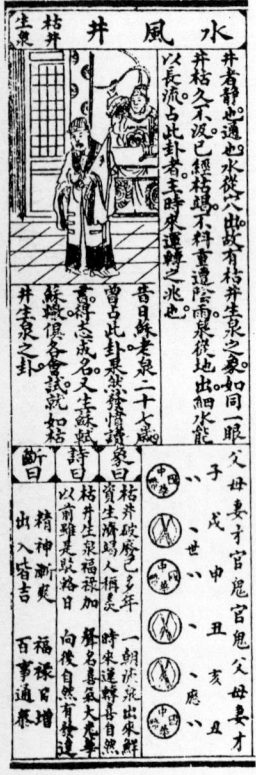

Thirtieth Hexagram 'The spring gushes up again in the bottom of the well in the oasis'

Symbol
A dried up well has been abandoned for a long time.
Suddenly one fine day a fresh spring erupts.
Rendering service to all and admired by all.
When a miracle occurs, nature herself rejoices.

Poem
The gushing of a new well increases happiness and prosperity:
Its good reputation and atmosphere of joy is made known everywhere.
Today the dark clouds have rolled away;
From now on everything will automatically become brilliant.

Auguries
The mind becomes more and more lucid.
Happiness and prosperity increase every day.
In your comings and goings you will always be happy.
For all your affairs go splendidly.

Apologue
During the Song dynasty, Su Laoquan, father of the famous poet Su Dongpo, did not learn to read until he was 27 years old. Despite this, however, he succeeded in rivalling his son.

Yi Jing 48th Hexagram *Jing* 'The well'
Trigrams Lower: 'Wind'
　　　　　　Upper: 'Water'

211112

Thirty-First Hexagram 'Dreaming of gold and silver in the night'

Symbol
Dreaming all night of gold and silver
Only to find yourself, on wakening, without a penny.
Today, be content with your fate:
Worrying about the morrow is futile.

Poem
The night's dreams have vanished when you awake.
It is hopeless to look for fame and riches.
Marriage will not be achieved and business is difficult.
Missing persons leave no trace.

Auguries
This month everything is topsy-turvy, and
All enterprises fail.
However, be patient in everything
And do not think too much about what might have been.

Apologue
Cao Cao (the celebrated villain of the *Romance of the Three Kingdoms*) believed he had found in Xu Shu a treasure of a counsellor, but he was never able to gain his services.

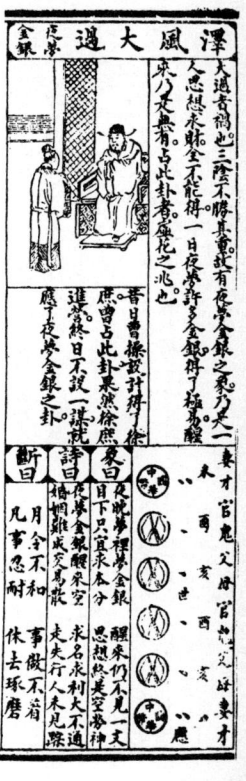

Yi Jing   28th Hexagram *Da guo* 'Excess'
Trigrams   Lower: 'Wind'
            Upper: 'Lake'

122112

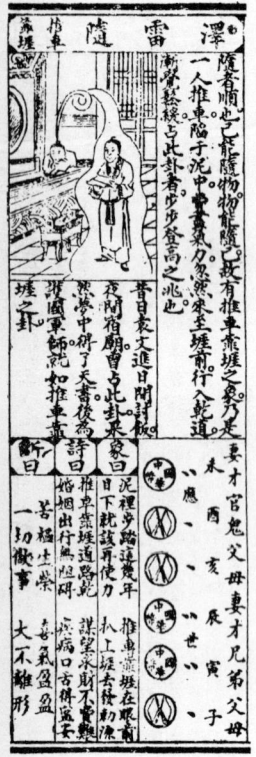

Thirty-Second Hexagram 'Pushing a wheelbarrow over parched soil'

Symbol
All these years one has plodded through the mud.
One pushes the wheelbarrow and suddenly one sees a dry track.
One more effort is needed to force the wheelbarrow onto the road.

Poem
If one pushes the wheelbarrow on a dry road,
Undertaking projects and searching for wealth do not seem impossible.
No obstacles are offered to marriages and travel.
Illness and quarrels will vanish of their own accord.

Auguries
An excess of misery engenders happiness.
Joy will be manifest everywhere.
In all things do not lose heart.

Apologue
The beggar, Yuan Wenjin, having found in a dream a book on celestial military art, worked hard at it and became a commander in chief.

Yi Jing   17th Hexagram *Sui* 'Agreement'
Trigrams   Lower: 'Thunder'
             Upper: 'Lake'

211211

Thirty-third Hexagram 'The grounded barge floats again'

Symbol
An isolated barge grounded on a sandy beach,
The poles stuck and useless, can neither move forwards nor backwards.
Rain comes and swells the flood:
Then, without effort, it drifts freely.

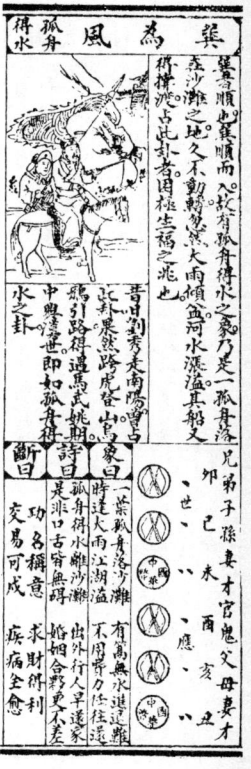

Poem
Once the water rises the barge can leave the sandbank.
Travellers can return home.
There are no more quarrels and misunderstandings
And harmony will reign in the household and between friends.

Auguries
Satisfying career.
Fortune assured.
Business prospers.
Illness completely cured.

Apologue
In his youth, fortified by this hexagram, the emperor, Quan Wu, of the Han dynasty succeeded in climbing a mountain without fear of walking over a tiger.

Yi Jing 57th Hexagram *Dun* 'Willing submission'
Trigrams Lower and Upper: 'Wind'
For Blofeld this hexagram is not entirely favourable.

79

111211

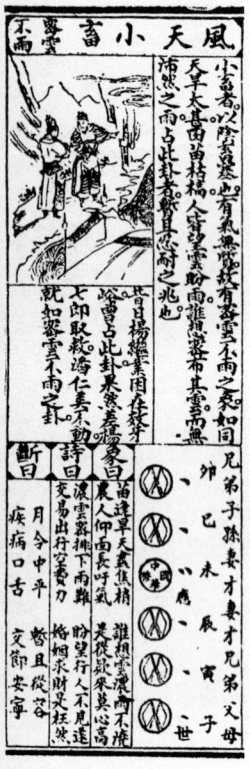

Thirty-Fourth Hexagram 'The cloudy sky gives no rain'

Symbol
Drought parches the grains of wheat.
Who would have thought that the sky could be covered with clouds without rain falling.
The peasants groan as they observe the sky.
Do not have too many illusions about yourself.

Poem
Although clouds cover the sky, no rain falls.
The travellers who are expected do not arrive.
Business and journeys are futile,
As futile as marriage and the quest for profit.

Auguries
A poor month.
You must be satisfied with what you have.
Illness and quarrels take time to be abated.

Apologue
General Yang Jiye, of the Song dynasty, who was captured by the enemy, begged his colleague General Pan Renmei to rescue him, only to meet with a refusal.

Yi Jing 9th Hexagram *Xiao shu* 'The lesser nourisher'
Trigrams Lower: 'Heaven'
Upper: 'Wind'
This hexagram is not a bad augury but it is of no immediate value.

121211

Thirty-Fifth Hexagram 'Contemplating a flower in the mirror'

Symbol
A lovely flower blooms in the mirror.
It is beautiful to look at but unobtainable.
Do not fall in love with the mirrored flower.
If you draw this hexagram, accept your bad luck.

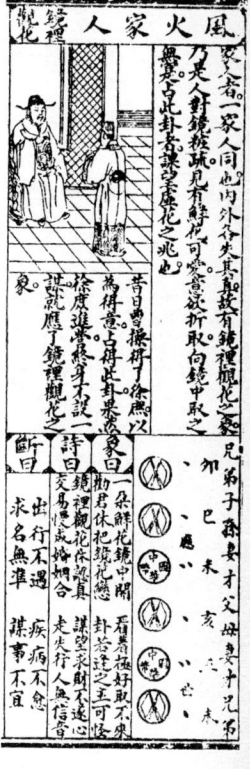

Poem
Do not take for real the flower you admire in the mirror.
You will not succeed in your quest for a fortune.
Business and marriage are unhappy.
No news from the traveller.

Auguries
Journeys will not fulfil your hopes.
Illness is still serious.
Uncertainty about careers.
Do not start any important enterprises.

Apologue
The notorious Cao Cao, having made the counsellor Xu Shu come to see him, thought he could benefit from his advice, but the latter consistently refused him.

Yi Jing 37th Hexagram *Jia ren* 'The Family'
Trigrams   Lower: 'Fire'
          Upper: 'Wind'
This hexagram is more favourable for women than for men.

81

122211

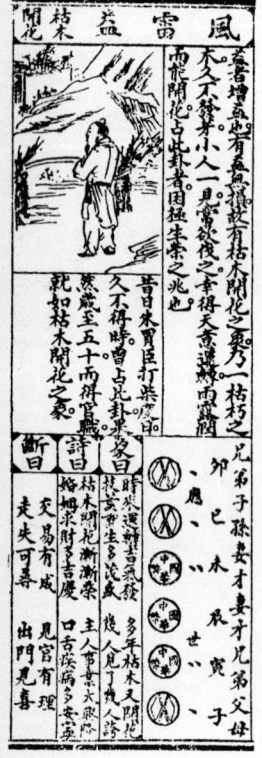

Thirty-Sixth Hexagram 'The withered tree flourishes again'

Symbol
The wheel of fortune has turned.
The tree, withered for many years, flourishes again.
Branches and leaves sprout in abundance.
Those who see it are filled with praise.

Poem
The tree which flourishes again becomes more and more prosperous.
Business is in full flow of expansion.
Marriage and affairs generally are all auspicious.
The quarrelsome are appeased and the sick cured.

Auguries
Business is full of success.
The lawsuit is won.
The missing are found.
Happiness knocks on the door.

Apologue
Zhu Maichen (Song dynasty) was a butcher but at the age of fifty he obtained a high dignity.

Yi Jing 42nd Hexagram *Yi* 'Gain'
Trigrams Lower: 'Thunder'
　　　　　Upper: 'Wind'

122111

Thirty-Seventh Hexagram 'A captive bird in its cage'

Symbol
The bird has fallen into the snare.
It tries without success to leave its cage.
It can only accept its fate,
Without trying to rise beyond the limits of possibility.

Poem
The bird in the cage cannot free itself.
Whoever draws this hexagram cannot do what he wants.
To make a fortune is most unlikely.
Illness and quarrels cause much anxiety.

Auguries
Journeys do not achieve their hoped for ends.
No profit from agreements.
No success in marriage.
Illness is past curing.

Apologue
Wen Wang, father of the first emperor of the Zhou dynasty (end of the twelfth century BC), was condemned without cause by the tyrant Zhou Wang and was kept in prison for a long time like a bird in a cage.

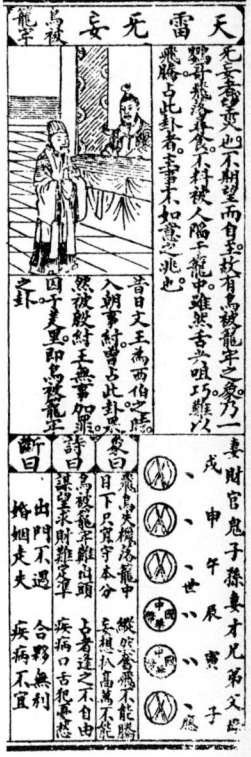

Yi Jing 25th Hexagram *Wu wang* 'Integrity, the Unexpected'
Trigrams Lower: 'Thunder'
            Upper: 'Heaven'
Blofeld notes that the title of this hexagram has two very different meanings which often co-exist in Chinese in the interpretations given to a hexagram. This hexagram is unfavourable only if one is in a state of uncertainty.

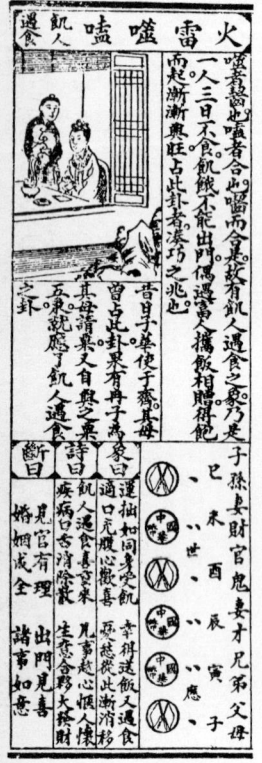

Thirty-Eighth Hexagram 'The starving find nourishment'

Symbol
When fate is unfavourable, one is like a starving person.
But then someone offers food and hunger is satisfied.
When the belly is full the heart is light,
And cares and sadness diminish little by little.

Poem
With nourishment the starving person recovers his joie de vivre.
He is happy for everything responds to his desires.
Illness and quarrelling disappear.
Business will certainly win a fortune.

Auguries
In court the lawsuit is won.
On leaving the house happiness is met.
Marriage is completely successful.
Everything is done according to your wishes.

Apologue
The mother of Zi Hua (Qi dynasty: there were two of this name in the fifth and sixth centuries AD) could get food only through her friends. This hexagram helped her to foresee it.

Yi Jing   21st Hexagram *Shi he* 'Gnawing'
Trigrams   Lower: 'Thunder'
                Upper: 'Fire'

122221

Thirty-Ninth Hexagram 'Pay a visit to the sages'

Symbol
The sage Tai Gong fished alone in the river Wei,
Holding in his hand a rod.
Wen Wang arrived unexpectedly to pay him a visit.
He will have no more difficulties for the rest of his life.
(See 37th Hexagram.)

Poem
King Wen visited the sage on the banks of the Wei.
Your search for riches will succeed.
Commerce and journeys will be satisfactory.
Illness and quarrels disappear.

Auguries
This visit to the sage on the river bank
Is a symbol of happiness and prosperity.
If you draw this hexagram,
How great your luck is.

Apologue
Zhuge Liang (*Romance of the Three Kingdoms*, see 28th Hexagram) received a visit from three generals of whom one was Guan Gong (16th Hexagram) who knew the quality of his strategy. As a consequence he became a generalissimo.

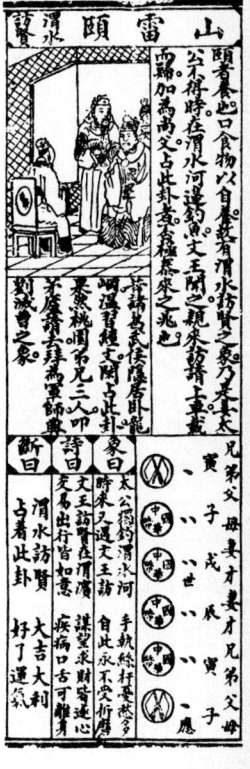

Yi Jing   27th Hexagram *Yi* 'Nourishment'
Trigrams   Lower: 'Thunder'
             Upper: 'Mountain'
The word nourishment should not be taken in its literal sense only.

211221

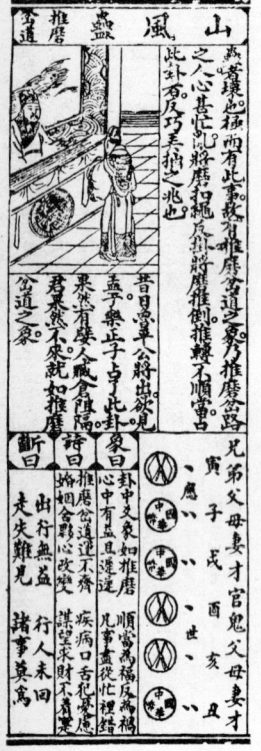

Fortieth Hexagram 'Pushing a millstone on a bumpy path'

Symbol

This hexagram evokes the example of the millstone which one wants to move.
That which should bring prosperity produces misery in the end.
The anxious heart hesitates and stops.
All evils come from excessive haste.

Poem

Luck does not smile on whoever pushes a millstone on a bumpy path.
Illness and quarrels cause concern.
Our partners change their minds.
The search for money is futile.

Auguries

Journeys are a dead loss.
Travellers do not arrive.
Missing persons have little chance of being found.
Abstain from everything.

Apologue

Mencius, the celebrated disciple of Confucius, was unable to meet prince Ping of Lu because a favourite opposed it.

Yi Jing   18th Hexagram *Gu* 'Decay'
Trigrams   Lower: 'Wind'
               Upper: 'Mountain'
The situation is only temporary; in fact this hexagram is an augury of success.

121121

Forty-First Hexagram 'The Celestial Mandarin brings happiness'

Symbol
The official who draws this hexagram will be given an important promotion.
Farmers will see their family fortunes increase.
Businessmen are assured of large profits.
Artisans will know prosperity.

Poem
Whoever draws this hexagram meets the Celestial Mandarin.*
Happiness and prosperity descend on earth.
Hopes and projects will bring joy.
Peace replaces cares and sadness.

*One of the Three Stars of Destiny, the spirit of happiness.

Auguries
The whole month is happy.
All affairs are in good shape.
Happiness appears at the threshold of the door.
Catastrophes and illness disappear.

Apologue
In spite of being a beggar, Lü Mengzhen came first in the imperial examinations.

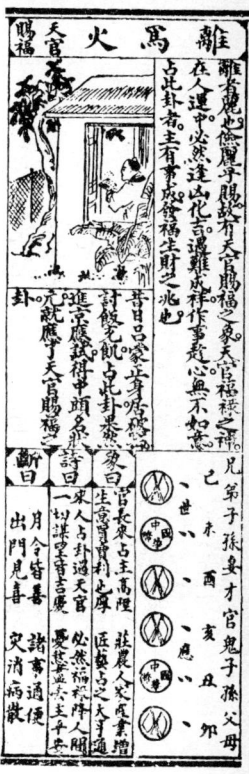

Yi Jing 30th Hexagram *Li* 'Flaming Beauty'
Trigrams Lower and Upper: 'Fire'

221121

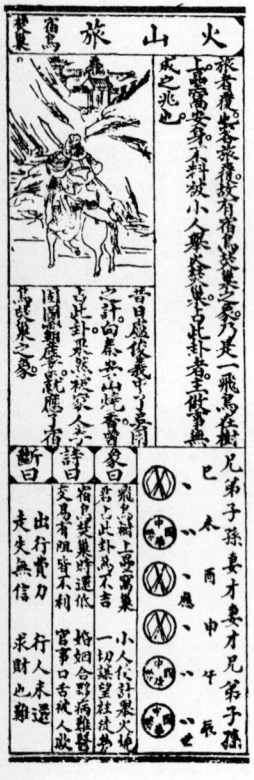

Forty-Second Hexagram 'The burnt bird's nest'

Symbol
Birds build their nests in the trees.
Some wicked people find a way of setting them on fire.
Whoever draws this hexagram truly has no luck,
And all his projects will founder.

Poem
When the birds return they find their nests burnt up.
There is danger in everything: marriage, partnerships, illness.
Business runs into obstacles which prevent all profit.
In lawsuits and quarrels you will be made a fool of.

Auguries
Journeys are a pointless effort.
Travellers do not arrive.
No news of absent ones.
Money is hard to get.

Apologue
Lu Junyi (Song dynasty) went to make a pilgrimage to Mount Tai. His servant profited by his absence to make away with all his goods.

Yi Jing 56th Hexagram *Lü* 'The traveller'
Trigrams Lower: 'Mountain'
Upper: 'Fire'

211121

Forty-Third Hexagram 'The fisherman makes a profit'

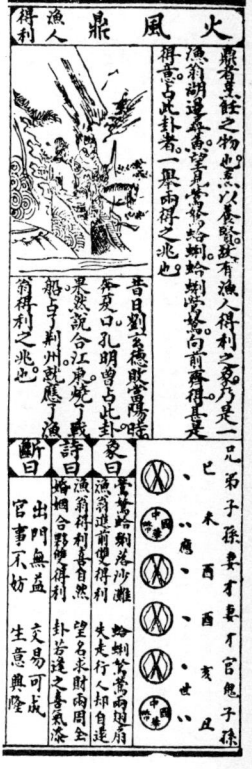

Symbol
Two birds have fallen on a sandy beach.
They try to spread their wings without being able to fly.
The old fisherman comes upon them and makes a double profit.
Those who have disappeared return.

Poem
Like the happy fisherman getting his double profit,
You will succeed in your career and fortune.
Marriage and business will be profitable.
To draw this hexagram is a sign of luck.

Auguries
It is not useful to leave the house.
Enterprises have a chance of success.
Lawsuits will not be opposed.
Business prospers.

Apologue
Liu Bei (*Romance of the Three Kingdoms*) took advantage of the battle between Cao Cao and the Wei to seize the city of Jingzhou.

Yi Jing   50th Hexagram *Ding* 'A sacrificial vessel'
Trigrams   Lower: 'Wind'
             Upper: 'Fire'

212121

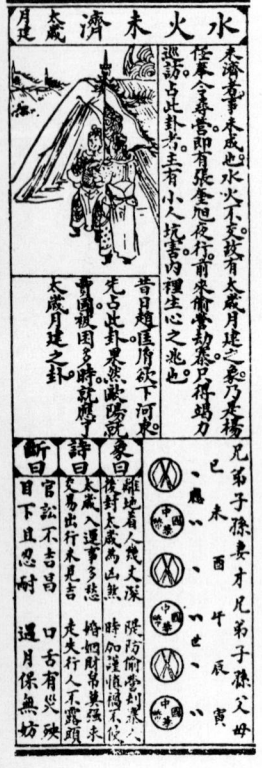

Forty-Fourth Hexagram 'Under the sign of the planet Jupiter'

Symbol
If you are on a floor several metres above the ground,
Beware of burglars entering during the night.
Jupiter is a maleficent planet.
So that only by taking great care will you avoid disaster.

Poem
When Jupiter marks your destiny, everything is a source of anxiety.
Do not try to press your luck in matters of marriage or money.
No luck on journeys
You will not see those you seek.

Auguries
Lawsuits are not favourable.
Quarrels turn to disaster.
For the time being be patient.
Obstacles disappear at the end of the month.

Apologue
The first emperor of the Song dynasty remained besieged as a consequence of the treachery of Ouyang Jing.

Yi Jing 64th Hexagram *Wei ji* 'Before Completion'
Trigrams Lower: 'Water'
Upper: 'Fire'

212221

Forty-Fifth Hexagram 'The little rascals steal money'

Symbol
This hexagram brings little luck to whoever draws it, for
It hints at troubles.
In your relationships numerous upsets.
In everything sorrow and fatigue.

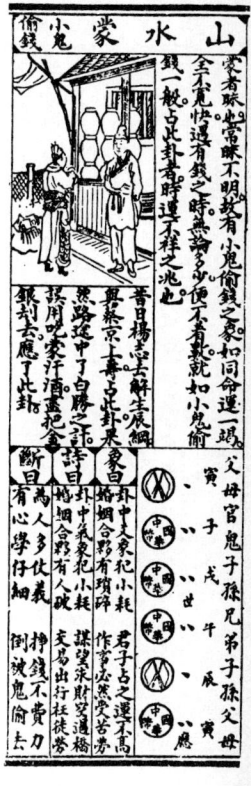

Poem
The minor losses indicated
Prove that you will be deceived if you try to enrich yourself.
Marriage and partnerships will be broken by third parties.
Business and journeys will be futile.

Auguries
You have been too generous,
Money having been easy to earn.
However vigilant you are,
You will be taken in by little rascals.

Apologue
General Yang Zhi of the Song dynasty was charged with conveying a large sum of money for the celebrations of the birthday of the prime minister. On the way he drank some wine drugged by a street urchin and all the money was stolen.

Yi Jing   4th Hexagram *Meng* 'Immaturity'
Trigrams   Lower: 'Water'
             Upper: 'Mountain'

212211

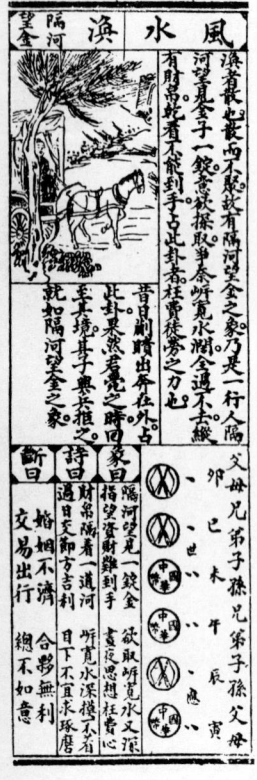

Forty-sixth Hexagram 'To gaze at gold from the other side of the river'

Symbol
To gaze at gold on the other bank of the river
When the river is too wide and the water too deep to seize it,
Is like a fortune within one's reach which one cannot grasp.
Think of it at night and the day will change nothing.

Poem
When the treasure is on the other bank and the stream is wide and the water deep,
Once the season has passed one will be happier.
For the moment try nothing.

Auguries
No success in marriage.
No luck with your partners.
Trade and travel will bring nothing.
Nothing will go as you wish it to.

Apologue
Kuai Kui (a contemporary of Confucius) wished to return to his own country but was opposed by his son with an army.

Yi Jing 59th Hexagram *Huan* 'Dispersed'
Trigrams Lower: 'Water'
Upper: 'Wind'
This hexagram presages success if one has enough patience to wait for it.

92

212111

Forty-Seventh Hexagram 'Two men dispute the passage'

Symbol
If one has projects in mind, it will be hard to realise them.
It is just like two men disputing a passage:
Each wishes to pass the other
And refuses to let the other pass him.

Poem
Two persons argue but neither wishes to give in.
Whoever draws this hexagram will have difficulties.
In business or on journeys obstacles will be met.
With partners results are poor.

Auguries
For the moment nothing works;
It is useless to worry.
Good things are hard to achieve,
But it is illusory to seek riches.

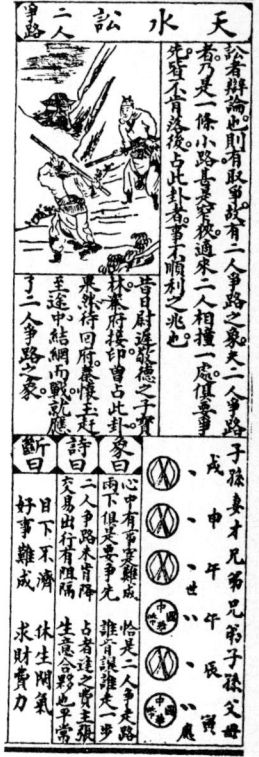

Apologue
Bao Ling, the son of general Hu Jingde, before carrying the imperial seal to his father, had to fight to keep it (Tang dynasty).

Yi Jing   6th Hexagram *Song* 'Conflict'
Trigrams   Lower: 'Water'
             Upper: 'Heaven'

121111

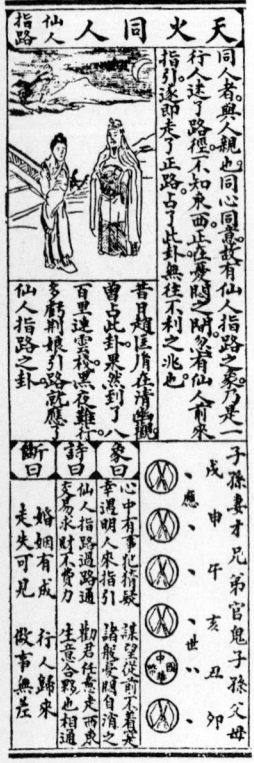

Forty-Eighth Hexagram 'The immortal shows the way'

Symbol
When one has matters at heart one hesitates.
One does not know how to realise the plans one has formed.
Luckily a clairvoyant shows us the way
And anxieties and cares disappear.

Poem
When the immortal shows us the way, all roads are open.
You can go as you will to the East or West.
In business no effort is necessary.
All goes well with your partners.

Auguries
Success in marriage.
The traveller arrives.
Missing persons are seen again.
All affairs will be perfect.

Apologue
Zhao Kuangyin (who became the first Song emperor) was lost one dark night and could only find his way again with the help of the Lady Jing.

Yi Jing 13th Hexagram *Tong ren* 'Lovers'
Trigrams Lower: 'Fire'
   Upper: 'Heaven'

222222

Forty-Ninth Hexagram 'The hungry tiger finds its nourishment'

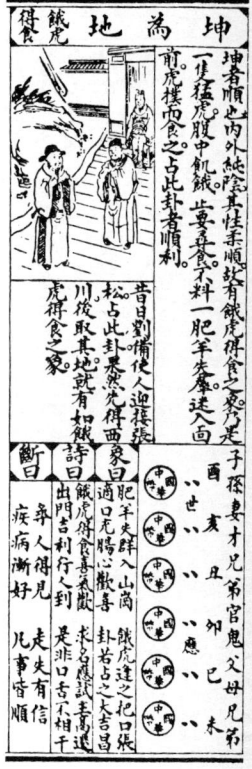

Symbol
The fat sheep separated from its flock wanders in the mountains.
A hungry tiger meets it and has only to open its jaws,
And fill its paunch to its heart content.

Poem
The hungry tiger is happy to have found its prey.
The candidates in the examinations will rise in rank.
The traveller will be happy.
Quarrels and gossip will not concern you.

Auguries
You will find the one you seek.
You will have news of the person who has disappeared.
Illness will improve.
Everything is favourable.

Apologue
Liu Bei (*Romance of the Three Kingdoms*) met Zhang Song who gave him a map of Sichuan province by means of which he conquered the territory.

Yi Jing 2nd Hexagram *Kun* 'The passive principle'
Trigrams Lower and Upper: 'Earth'

122222

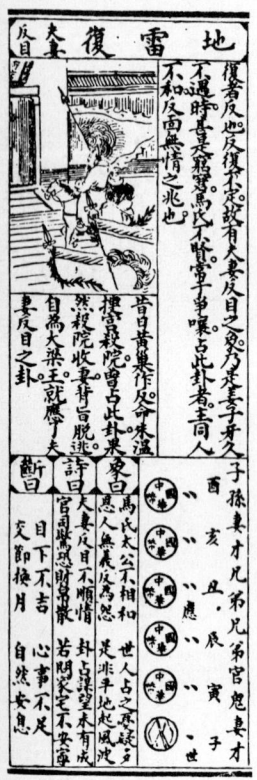

Fiftieth Hexagram 'Discord between husband and wife'

Symbol
Two spouses do not understand each other.
Whoever draws this hexagram will have a lot of bother.
The friend becomes an enemy.
Over the earth the wind inexplicably blows up into a tempest.

Poem
When spouses quarrel no peace is possible.
Whoever draws this hexagram will find it hard to realise his projects.
Lawsuits are disquieting and riches vanish.
The whole family knows peace no longer.

Auguries
For the moment no happiness.
Your desires are not achievable.
You must wait for the month to pass away,
When peace and calm will return automatically.

Apologue
Huang Chao (Tang dynasty period), who came top in the imperial examinations, rebelled against the emperor and massacred the whole court.

Yi Jing   24th Hexagram *Fu* 'Return'
Trigrams   Lower: 'Thunder'
             Upper: 'Earth'

112222

Fifty-First Hexagram 'Benevolence in the government'

Symbol
When the king does not follow the right path, the people hang their heads in shame.
They hope the clouds will pass in order to see the sun;
But if they find a master who conducts a benevolent government,
They recover the joy of living in peace.

Poem
When there is benevolence in government, sentiments become noble.
One can travel freely to enrich oneself.
Relationships and marriage bring hope to all.
Those who are absent and travellers will give their news.

Auguries
Quarrels will lead to lawsuits.
The illness will improve slowly.
Careers are satisfactory.
Peace and tranquillity reign at home.

Apologue
The beggar Gao Huaide met Zhao Kuangyin and they became blood brothers. When the latter became emperor, Gao obtained titles and wealth.

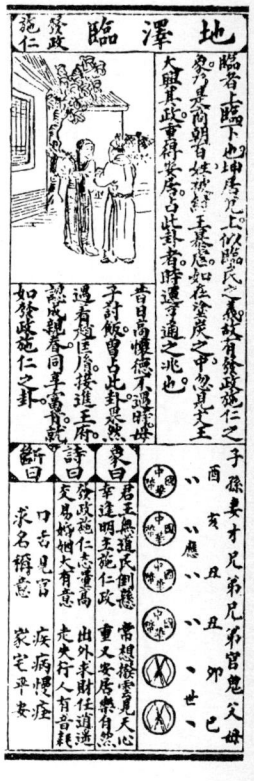

Yi Jing   19th Hexagram *Lin* 'Approach'
Trigrams   Lower: 'Lake'
            Upper: 'Earth'

111222

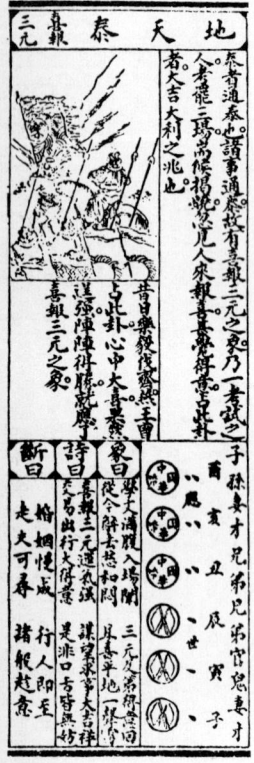

Fifty-Second Hexagram 'The proud announcement for success in three examinations'

Symbol
Having worked one's hardest, one enters the examination hall,
Comes first thrice and returns home entirely happy.
From now on grief and cares depart and
Exuberant joy fills the earth.

Poem
What luck to have come first;
It is an augury of good fortune in all your enterprises.
Business and travel will give full satisfaction.
Neither gossip nor quarrels will trouble you.

Auguries
Marriage is only accomplished slowly.
Travellers are going to arrive.
You will find the one you are looking for.
All will come about according to your wishes.

Apologue
Having drawn this hexagram, the King of Yan is everywhere victorious (fourth century AD).

Yi Jing 11th Hexagram *Tai* 'Peace'
Trigrams Lower: 'Heaven'
　　　　　 Upper: 'Earth'

111122

Fifty-Third Hexagram 'The carpenter finds the appropriate wood'

Symbol
A worker finds a suitable piece of wood.
He takes it and goes on his way.
When luck turns everything becomes easy.
Whatever one does will be successful.

Poem
After his find the carpenter is filled with joy.
Business and enterprises all will succeed.
Marriage and partnerships respond to your wishes.
Everything you undertake will succeed.

Auguries
Favourable journeys.
Quarrels avoided.
Illness is cured.
The traveller arrives.

Apologue
Having dreamt of a flying bear, the King of Jin drew this hexagram and then met general Li Cunxiao. Thanks to his help he was able to bring about the triumph of the Tang dynasty (seventh century AD).

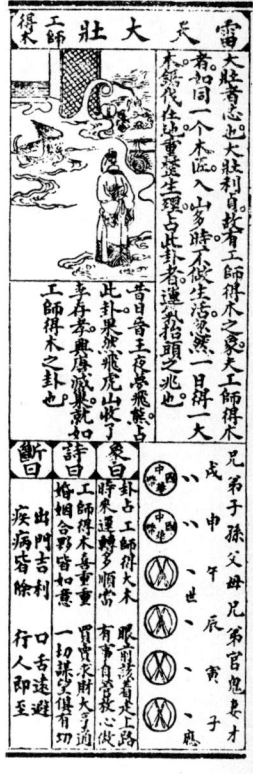

Yi Jing   34th Hexagram *Da zhuang* 'The power of the great'
Trigrams   Lower: 'Heaven'
             Upper: 'Thunder'

111112

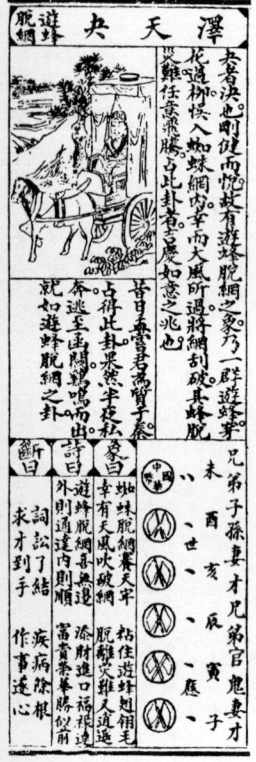

Fifty-Fourth Hexagram 'The fluttering bee escapes from the spider's web'

Symbol
A spider's web is like a celestial prison;
A fluttering bee finds itself caught in it.
Luckily a breath of wind breaks the web.
It can escape from danger and recover its freedom.

Poem
This liberated bee represents unlimited happiness.
Riches come as well as happiness and honours.
Harmony at home, good understanding outside.
The past is eclipsed by today.

Auguries
The lawsuit comes to an end.
Illness is completely cured.
You will get rich and
Everything will go as you wish.

Apologue
Meng Changjun (*Romance of the Three Kingdoms*) successfully fled his country in order to avoid imprisonment.

Yi Jing   43rd Hexagram *Guai* 'Resolution'
Trigrams   Lower: 'Heaven'
             Upper: 'Lake'

111212

Fifty-Fifth Hexagram 'A brilliant pearl emerges from the earth'

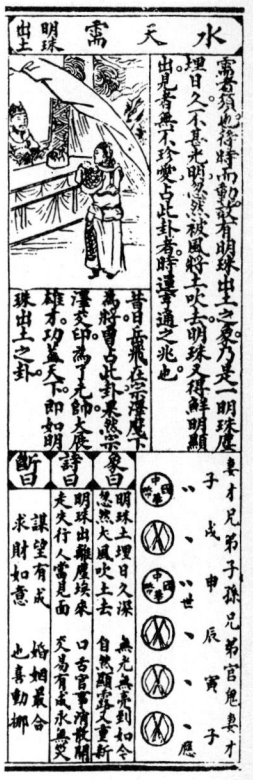

Symbol
A brilliant pearl has been buried for a long time.
Until today neither its splendour nor its orient was known.
Suddenly a gust of wind blows away the dust.
And the pearl appears in all its splendour.

Poem
When the brilliant pearl emerges from the dust,
Quarrels and litigation fade away.
Absent ones return.
Unmixed success in one's affairs.

Auguries
Success in all our projects.
Marriage is very harmonious.
Wealth according to our desires.
Energy must be displayed.

Apologue
In his early days Yue Fei (*Romance of the Three Kingdoms*) was unknown to his superiors. Zong Ze learned to appreciate him and appointed him commander in chief.

Yi Jing 5th Hexagram *Xu* 'Calculated inaction'
Trigrams Lower: 'Heaven'
            Upper: 'Water'

222212

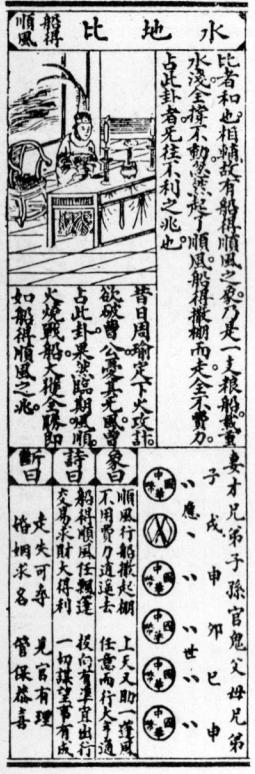

Fifty-Sixth Hexagram 'A favourable wind for embarkation'

Symbol
When the wind is propitious the boat hoists its sail,
And the sky helps too by stiffening the breeze.
Without effort, go as you please and wherever you wish.

Poem
When the ship gets a favourable wind, she goes freely towards her destination.
If one is sure of one's direction, travel is favoured.
Full success will be achieved in relationships and business.
And your hopes will be fulfilled.

Auguries
Missing persons are found.
The lawsuit is won.
Marriage prospers.
Great success in your career.

Apologue
Zhou Yu (*Romance of the Three Kingdoms*), having obtained a favourable wind, was able to burn Cao Cao's fleet.

Yi Jing   8th Hexagram *Bi* 'Unity'
Trigrams   Lower: 'Earth'
               Upper: 'Water'

112112

Fifty-Seventh Hexagram 'Taking advantage of water to make mortar'

Symbol
This hexagram is truly interesting
For it helps you to find work without effort.
Do not miss the opportunity offered you
And everything will respond to your wishes.

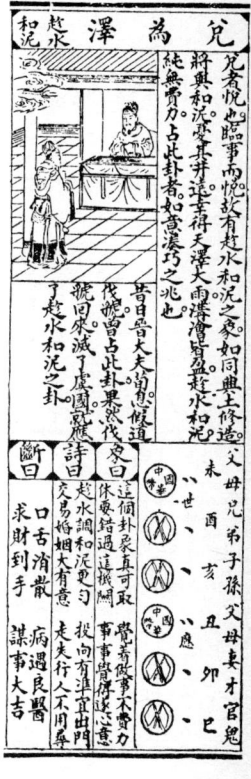

Poem
Water must be used to shape the mud.
If the wind is fair, travel is indicated.
Great satisfaction in partnerships and marriage.
It is futile to search for missing persons.

Auguries
Quarrels will blow away.
The invalid will find a good doctor.
The riches looked for will be obtained.
Good luck in business.

Apologue
Xun Xi, minister of the King of Jin, having drawn this hexagram conquered two neighbouring kingdoms.

Yi Jing   58th hexagram *Dui* 'Joy'
Trigrams   Lower and Upper: 'Lake'

212112

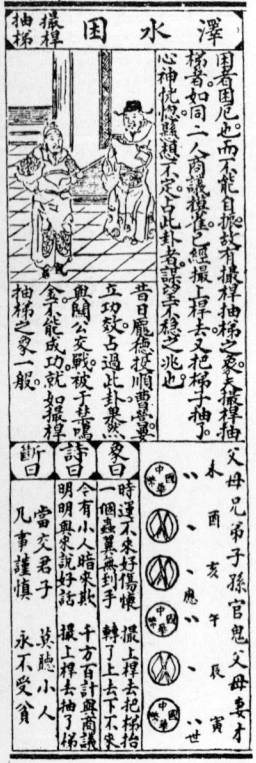

Fifty-Eighth Hexagram 'To reach out with a stick but remove the ladder'

Symbol
When there is no luck, how sad it is:
The stick has been extended but the ladder withdrawn.
Not a single insect has been caught;
And one can neither climb further nor descend.

Poem
There is a mean fellow who tries to fool one.
We discuss a thousand projects together
And his words are friendly;
But if he stretches out the stick to me, he removes the ladder.

Auguries
You should consort with well brought up people
And avoid the vulgar.
Be cautious in everything
And do not let yourself be corrupted.

Apologue
General Pang De (*Romance of the Three Kingdoms*) tried to fight a glorious action against Guan Gong (16th Hexagram), but he was prevented by a trick of one of his comrades who warned Guan Gong.

Yi Jing   47th Hexagram *Kun* 'Adversity'
Trigrams Lower: 'Water'
            Upper: 'Lake'

222112

Fifty-Ninth Hexagram 'The carp becomes a Dragon'

Symbol
The carp which plays in the water is frightened by the net.
It jumps over the Longmen pass and changes into a Dragon.*
The willows let fall the golden threads
And the flowers of the peach presage your fortune.

*(see p. 112, note 21.)

Poem
The metamorphosis of the carp brings a breath of happiness.
Quarrels and maladies disappear.
Doubts and cares are stemmed when the gate of unhappiness is closed
And the gate of joy is opened.

Auguries
Once the carp becomes a Dragon,
Happy events follow in succession.
You will obtain the wealth you sought
And accomplish your enterprises.

Apologue
Ban Chao (Han dynasty), having failed in the examinations, threw away his brushes and embraced a military career. After many victories he became a high dignitary.

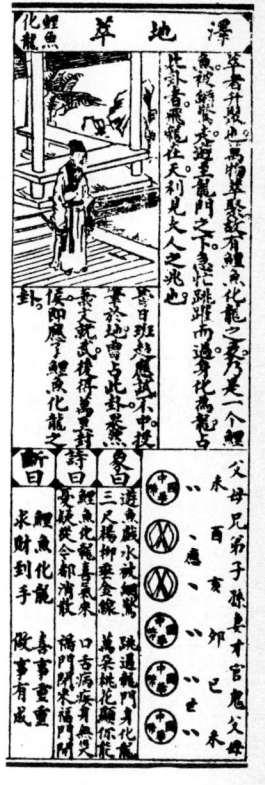

Yi Jing 45th Hexagram *Cui* 'Gathering together'
Trigrams Lower: 'Earth'
Upper: 'Lake'

221112

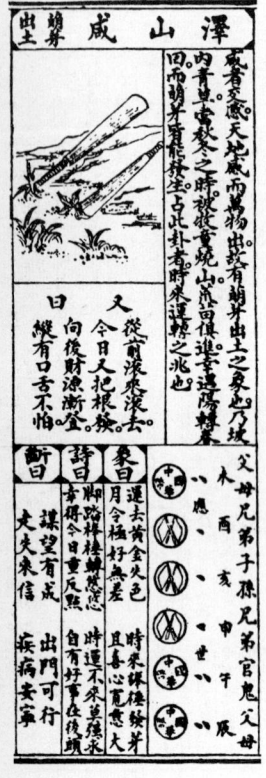

Sixtieth Hexagram 'The seeds sprout from the earth'

Symbol
When luck flies away, the yellow gold loses its colour.
In its own time the withered tree gives forth shoots.
Luck this month is good
Provided you have courage.

Poem
The withered plants sprout again,
But luck should never be forced.
Happily today is a turning point:
Soon happy events will come to pass.

Auguries
Projects are realised.
Travel will be possible.
Those absent will send news.
Invalids will find a cure.

Apologue
Frost is never decisive and seeds will always sprout in the Spring. (This apologue is the only one to take nature as an example.)

Yi Jing   31st Hexagram *Xian* 'Attraction'
Trigrams   Lower: 'Mountain'
              Upper: 'Lake'

221212

Sixty-First Hexagram 'Rain and snow obstruct the way'

Symbol
Torrential rain floods the roads, and snow fills the sky.
On the road the pedestrian suffers from misery and cold.
He is exhausted from floundering in the mud and water,
But he must be patient when things do not go as he would wish.

Poem
Rain and snow transform the road into a quagmire.
Relationships are unsure and journeys difficult.
Illness drags on and marriage is delayed.
No hope of earning money.

Auguries
Travellers do not arrive.
It is hard to find the way in which one should go.
You are disoriented.
Career is uncertain.

Apologue
Han Yu (Tang dynasty) set out in search of a friend, but he found the passes blocked by snow and was forced to give up.

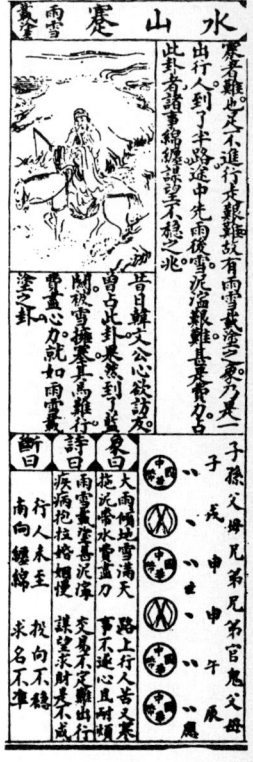

Yi Jing   39th Hexagram *Jian* 'Trouble'
Trigrams   Lower: 'Mountain'
              Upper: 'Water'
This hexagram is a sign of difficulty or imminent danger.

107

221222

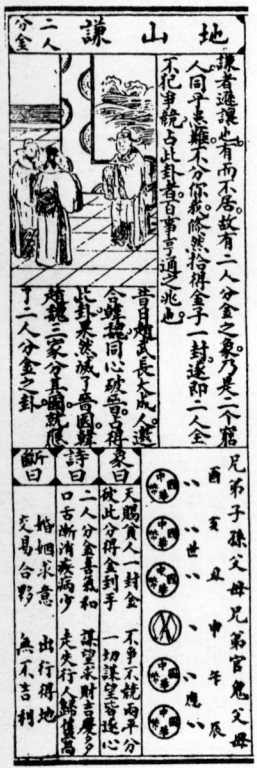

Sixty-Second Hexagram 'Two men share the treasure'

Symbol
Heaven has helped the poor to find treasure.
Without quarrelling, two men divide it equitably.
Each has his share of the gold
And their plans can be realised.

Poem
Those who share with such harmony
Will find fortune and happiness,
And quarrels and illness will be rare.
Lost travellers return to the fold.

Auguries
Satisfactory marriage.
Advantageous journeys.
Advantageous business.
Everything arrives at the right moment.

Apologue
Having drawn this hexagram, Zhao Wu decided to get help from the Kingdoms of Han and of Wei in order to conquer the Kingdom of Qin.

Yi Jing 15th Hexagram *Qian* 'Modesty'
Trigrams Lower: 'Mountain'
            Upper: 'Earth'

221122

Sixty-Third Hexagram 'To rush over a plank bridge'

Symbol
The pedestrian crosses a bridge made of a single plank.
He is nervous and has a fixed look on his face.
If one crosses quickly, one will succeed without difficulty:
But if one hesitates one will never cross.

Poem
It is hard to walk on a single plank bridge,
For it makes the head swim.
Trade and business generally must be concluded quickly;
And to succeed, the bridegroom must not be late.

Auguries
You will get the money you want.
The lawsuit will end without trouble.
For the moment not everything is perfect,
But in time all will be well.

Apologue
Threatened with death by his cousin, Han Tui, Confucius left quickly for the Kingdom of Song.

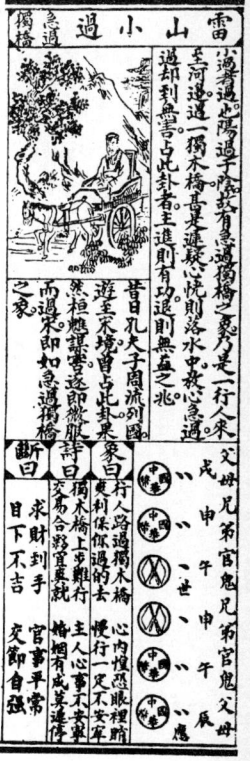

Yi Jing 62nd Hexagram *Xiao guo* 'The small get by'
Trigrams Lower: 'Mountain'
Upper: 'Thunder'

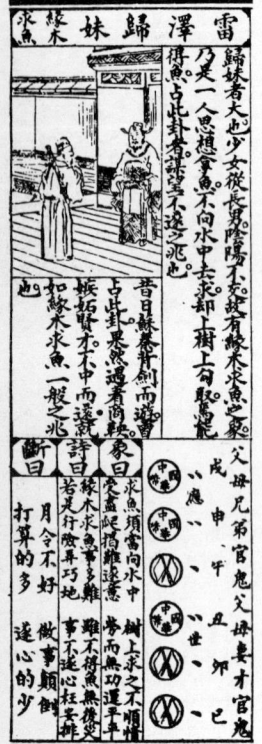

Sixty-Fourth Hexagram 'To climb a tree to catch a fish'

Symbol
Fishing can only be done in water.
It is stupid to clamber up a tree.
There is every chance of not getting what one wants.
Destiny is inglorious and mediocre.

Poem
To look for fish up a tree is an impossible enterprise,
But it is not important whether one succeeds or not.
If one thinks oneself smarter than others
One will succeed in nothing that one does.

Auguries
The whole month is bad.
Business is at sixes and sevens.
Projects are many but few succeed.
The heart is unsatisfied.

Apologue
Once the jurist Su Qin met his rival Shang Yang who, jealous of the other's talent, refused to make use of it. He might just as well have looked for a fish in a tree.

Yi Jing 54th Hexagram *Gui mei* 'The marriageable maiden'
Trigrams Lower: 'Lake'
Upper: 'Thunder'
From the beginning of any action it is necessary to understand what mistakes to avoid.

Notes

1 *Les Huits Signes de votre Destin*, Paris, L'Asiathèque, 1981 and *The Way to Chinese Astrology – The Four Pillars of Destiny*, Unwin Paperbacks, 1983. (Referred to as *Four Pillars* in notes below.)
2 *I Ching: The Book of Change*, by John Blofeld, Unwin paperbacks, 1978. On the importance of the *Yi Jing*, see *Four Pillars*, pp. 49–50.
3 On the oracular inscriptions found at Anyang (Henan), see *Four Pillars*, p. 137, note 13. I have since discovered that the two series of cyclic characters, denary and duodenary, were already in use at this time: 甲骨文選讀 Jiaguwen xuan du (*Study of a Selection of Oracular Inscriptions*), Shanghai, 1981, p. 35.
4 不知命無以為君子也 see Legge, *The Chinese Classics*, Vol. 1, p. 354. It goes without saying that I assume entire responsibility for my translation which is very different from his.
5 The role of the Emperor, the intermediary par excellence between Earth and Heaven, was primarily to maintain the Universal (天下) Order. By publishing the calendar and by the control of weights and measures, he ruled time and space. It is significant that the Throne Room in the Imperial Palace in Beijing (Peking) was called 'Hall of Supreme Harmony'.
6 The teachings of Confucius are a collection of rules and moral principles: the virtue (which above all signifies conformity with natural law) of the Prince derives the rule of Order in the Empire. As for spirits (and the cult of ancestors), Confucius felt that traditions should be followed; but, since it was impossible to know anything about them, he thought it pointless to discuss the subject. *Four Pillars* p. 7.
7 The Chinese are never as concerned about their personal safety as they are with the continuity of the family. It was very much in this spirit that Mao Zedong felt that there was no need to fear a nuclear war, for there would always be enough Chinese survivors to perpetuate the race.
8 *Four Pillars*, pp. 15–16.
9 *Four Pillars*, p. 14 and p. 137, note 13.
10 I have already mentioned the translation by John Blofeld. Some texts dated 168 BC which have been discovered in Hunan province, at Mawangdui near Changsha, include notably a text of the *Yi Jing*. When this text is published it will furnish some interesting points and will perhaps help to improve existing translations.
11 Copper coins, pierced with a square hole, were used in China as small change, often strung together. The coppers were believed to chase away evil spirits and are therefore auspicious. Taoist priests combatted demons with the help of magic swords made of copper coins firmly tied together. Three copper coins are often used instead of sticks to cast the Hexagrams of the *Yi Jing*.
12 In French the term used for these coins is *sapèques* for which I can find no suitable English equivalent. However, the coins used in China for divinatory purposes were made of copper or brass, with a square hole in the middle, and were of very little value. In Chinese they were known as *tongzier* and

represented one cent of the old silver dollar, the common currency before the Second World War. To English-speaking foreigners the 'tongzier' were known as copper cash or simply 'coppers'. I have chosen to translate the word as penny which not only describes a coin of low denomination still in general circulation, but is also loosely used for 'money' and sometimes even in a quasi-magical sense, e.g. 'pennies from heaven'! (See also note 11.)

13 Allegories and apologues are based on more or less historical recitals such as *The Romance of the Three Kingdoms*, and *The Water Margin* popularised by storytellers, singers and by the theatre. They are as well known in China as were the *Chansons de Geste* and Mystery plays in medieval Europe.

14 In his chapter 4, Blofeld similarly underlines the importance of taking the interrogation of the oracle seriously.

15 People are also firmly discouraged from interrogating the oracles on certain days, particularly the lunar New Year's Day. If they happen to visit a pagoda on such a day it would be improper and discourteous to take advantage of the occasion to consult the oracle. Likewise, as a matter of courtesy, a visitor in China never reveals the purpose of his visit the first time he calls on you.

16 Geometrical figures traced on the ground by Tibetan monks which help concentration of the mind and therefore contemplation.

17 Granet, *La Pensée Chinoise*, pp. 154–5.

18 *Four Pillars*, pp. 82 and 78.

19 According to Chinese tradition, the appearance of these mythical animals is extremely auspicious. The Phoenix, which symbolises the Empress as opposed to the Dragon for the Emperor, only shows itself in periods of peace and prosperity. The Unicorn bring long life and happiness.

20 It will be noted that in the first line of the poem the second ideogram has been left out. It ought to be the word *ge*, fourth character of the title; but since it means 'revolution' as well as 'change' it has quite simply been suppressed in almanacs published in Taiwan and Hongkong.

21 *Longmen* ('Dragon's Gate') is the name of some rapids in the Yellow River. The legend says that the carp which can clear them will be transformed into a dragon; whence the practice of serving carp as a token of good luck, if a candidate in the examinations is invited to dinner.

22 It is not the orientation towards the South which is auspicious, but the too great heat which results from it.

23 In order to understand this rather surprising oracle, it must be remembered that it does not speak about your luck generally; but simply advises you to be patient: your question is premature!

24 See note 23 to the Sixth Pentagram. This text applies only to the question asked. If one reads the response in the light of the poem, the burden of its advice is prudence for the time being.

25 The isle of Penglai in the Eastern Sea is the residence and meeting place of immortals.

26 This phrase is rather obscure but I think it should be understood in the sense of note 19 to the First Pentagram: the Dragon and the Phoenix appear only in times of peace.

27 An allusion to the traditional family feast of the Moon which occurs on the fifteenth day of the eighth lunar month.

28 Happiness and Honour are two of the three stars of destiny, the third being

longevity which, even if not named, is always implied when the other two are mentioned.
29 This is not a high philosophic theme, but a Confucian idea that if a man achieves harmony within himself it will react on the universe and vice versa.
30 See note 12 on the use of the word 'penny'. 'Golden' here is used euphemistically.
31 *Four Pillars*, pp. 54–5. In this text I have used the word 'movement' to describe the six energies. However, I think that the term 'energy' used by acupuncturists is more precise for it avoids confusion with the five terrestrial movements.

Glossary

ACUPUNCTURE A means of restoring the balance of the energies in the body by the use of needles. It is incorrect to describe acupuncture as a mere form of therapy.

AGENTS (the Five) The Five Agents are Wood, Fire, Earth, Metal, Water and they represent the fundamental manifestation of Energy (q.v.) The Agents can be either Yin or Yang (see *Four Pillars*, chapters 7, 12, 13).

APOLOGUE An allegorical story intended to convey a useful lesson: e.g., fable, parable.

ASTROLOGY A form of divination (q.v.) based on a study of the movements of heavenly bodies.
1 Some people believe that the stars influence human behaviour (e.g., the Chaldeans, the Romans); this is true astrology.
2 Others, like the Chinese, use the stars simply to calculate the calendar. Chinese astrology should be more properly called 'CHRONO-MANCY' or numerology based on time.

AUGURY The conclusion or significant elements in an oracle (q.v.).

DIVINATION Any system which tries to predict the future.

EIGHT SIGNS (or characters) OF DESTINY Popular name for the Four Pillars (q.v.) each of which consists of two characters.

ENERGY The Chinese consider energies to be the very essence of the Universe, a view quite close to that of modern physics. This Energy, which emanates from Dao (Tao), the law of nature, is expressed in two opposing yet complementary principles: Yin and Yang (q.v.).

ENERGIES (Celestial – Six) Also known as the three Yang and three Yin. The name given to Energy in relation to Earth.

FOUR PILLARS OF DESTINY The four binomials: for the year, the month, the day and the hour which define each moment. Equivalent to the Eight Signs.

HEXAGRAMS The sixty-four possible combinations of trigrams (q.v.) which are represented by broken (Yin) and unbroken (Yang) lines, or by heads or tails when coins are used as in this book.

HOROSCOPE Definition of the character of a person depending on his time of birth. To the Chinese the purpose of a horoscope is not to predict the future but to help him to understand himself.

IDEOGRAM A character or figure symbolising the idea without expressing the name of it: e.g., the Chinese characters. In the West, the figures 1, 2, 3 etc. are ideograms.

LI Chinese measure of distance which varied in different parts of China and in different epochs, but in modern times is generally taken to be equal to one third of a mile.

MANDALA   Geometric figures drawn on the ground by Tibetan Lamas with different coloured powders as an aid to the concentration necessary for meditation.

MOVEMENTS (Terrestrial – Five)   Name given to Energy (q.v.) in relation to Earth.

NADIR   Diametrically opposite to the Zenith; the point directly under the observer in relation with the four cardinal points. For the Chinese the nadir (centre) is the fifth cardinal point.

ORACLE   A judgement given by a soothsayer or the answer given in response to a divinatory enquiry.

PENTAGRAMS   Thirty-two figures formed by throwing five coins, which can be Yin or Yang depending on whether they are tails or heads. They can be represented by five lines, broken or unbroken, in the same way as hexagrams of the Yi Jing.

ROMANCE OF THE THREE KINGDOMS   An assembly of romantic tales ostensibly based on events in the second century AD. They are still very popular in China. They might very roughly be compared with the stories about King Arthur and the Knights of the Round Table.

TRIGRAMS   Eight figures composed of three lines which may be broken (Yin) or unbroken (Yang) or combinations of each. Each of the sixty-four hexagrams (q.v.) of the Yi Jing is composed of two trigrams.

YIN AND YANG   The two opposing yet complementary principles which represent the first manifestation of Energy (q.v.), often simplistically represented as the feminine and masculine, or the negative and positive aspects of Energy. They can be more accurately described as the phases of concentration (Yin) and expansion (Yang).